D1299484

knitovation

creative knitwear made from 3 simple shapes

Barry Klein & Fayla Reiss

knitovation

creative knitwear made from 3 simple shapes

Barry Klein & Fayla Reiss

This book is dedicated to all the knitters who love our art form and are inspired to learn more. Knit on!

233 Spring Street
New York, NY 10013

Library of Congress Control Number: 2005928638

ISBN 13: 978-1-931543-82-8
ISBN 10: 1-931543-82-8

Manufactured in China

1 3 5 7 9 8 6 4 2

table of contents

INTRODUCTION

We have all made tons of scarves. You start out with a few stitches and you knit every row, letting the yarns textures and colors show off. When only enough yarn remains to bind off, you are done. Can it be any simpler? With that basic idea in mind, we have designed a collection of sweaters, jackets, accessories and home fashions that are all based on keeping it simple and letting the yarn do the work. **Knitovation** will show you just how easy it is to knit something sensational out of three simple shapes: a square, a rectangle and a triangle.

The idea for this book came from Fayla. She's a magician, taking something flat and folding it into something shapely. Barry approaches designing using basic knitting techniques to create shapes that show off the yarns' textures to their fullest. Together, we combined our styles to bring you **Knitovation**.

Throughout this book, you will see that we set our goals high to create fabulous fashions for you and your home using these simple shapes and some innovative techniques. This book is meant to encourage and inspire the novice knitters using illustrations of theses shapes at the beginning of each project so you can see exactly what shapes you will be knitting. We will also take you through the techniques you will need to know to complete each of our designs, including how to fold and assemble pieces in new and unconventional ways to create fashions that will fit, flatter and feel great.

All of the techniques you learn here will also help you become a better, more experienced knitter and will open up your mind to new ideas. Most important, you will see how easy it is to take a simple shape and create something sophisticated. Whether you want to make something to wear or something to decorate your home, **Knitovation** will get you there with confidence. Let's go through this fun and easy journey together.

IN THE BEGINING

We began with the idea that you have the basic knitting techniques under control: how to cast on and bind off, and how to work in garter stitch and Stockinette stitch. If you've done one or more scarves, then to us, you are an expert and are ready to work with our patterns. Most of the designs in this book are created to take your knowledge of the basics and to move you forward. Each design will bring in a new idea or a new technique. In some cases, a simple yarn or color change will give you a fresh new look. In other instances we will have you folding the knitted pieces to create new shapes. This chapter will take you through the simple beginnings of getting started. If you're ready, so are we. Let's show you what **Knitovation** is all about!

The Shapes of Things To Come

We worked with the "KISS" principle: "Keep It Simple and Sophisticated." Another one of our goals was to show all of the new scarf knitters that there is really no difference between knitting a scarf and knitting a body piece. To accomplish this, we made the decision to work with pieces that are in most cases, not altered by decreasing and increasing stitches. In other words, you work straight from cast-on to bind-off. However, sometimes we shape pieces by changing needle sizes to get the shapes we want.

Throughout **Knitovation**, we will be working with three basic shapes: squares, rectangles and triangles. Look for these symbols at the beginning of each of the instructions. They will tell you the shape or shapes you will be making and how many of each you will need to complete the project.

A square has four right angle (90°) corners and all sides are equal. With knitting, the four sides are as close to equal in length and width as possible. However, it is not always easy to create a perfect square since many of the yarns that we use are stretchy. And with the method that we use for measuring (see Measuring Knitted Pieces on page 9), some things can look different hanging on a needle as opposed to resting on a flat surface. In all cases we give you measurements so that you can knit each square as a square. For some designs, we will be turning a square on one of its points to create a diamond.

A rectangle has four right angle corners like a square, but the length and width have different measurements...just like a scarf. For some projects, you will create a rectangle by knitting two squares and sewing them together.

A triangle has three angle corners (that are less than 90°) and three sides. To knit a triangle, you will need to either increase or decrease along the side edges to create the shape. Some of our triangles are worked from the bottom up, increasing at each side to the top edge. Others are knitted from the top down, decreasing at each side edge to the bottom point.

As we began putting the patterns together, Fayla would bring out sheets of paper and napkins or anything she could get her hands on. Because much of what we do involves moving and folding the knitted pieces, Fayla would cut and turn the paper pieces to show me how it all would come together. As a result, the ideas became truly visual and opened my eyes to all the possibilities ahead. So, we recommend that you keep some 8 squares = 1"/2.5cm graph paper handy. Using one grid to equal 1"/2.5cm, draw the finished sizes of the pattern pieces on the graph paper, then cut out. Use these mini paper pieces to help you see how the knitted pieces have to get put together. In addition, we have found that making life-size patterns out of fabric or felt helped in making sure that the knitted piece is done to size. If you use cut fabric as a template, you can place the knitted piece on top to see where you are.

Yarn Selections

If you are like us, the visual aspect is what has drawn you to knitting and the textures and colors add even more to the excitement. For each of the designs, we have carefully selected yarns for their textural quality, color schemes, ease in knitting and their drape on the body. One of our favorite things to do is to have our own personal "knit out" to better understand each of the yarns we want to use. We will take a whole group of yarns and lay them out. We spend hours just making swatches in different stitches, blending different yarns together to create new yarns and changing needle sizes to see how that will affect the look and feel of the yarn. Ultimately, we select the yarn or yarns that best highlight a design.

Gauge

Under normal circumstances, stitch gauge and row gauge are the most important part of achieving a perfect finished sweater and a perfect body fit. What we have achieved in Knitovation is to make gauge a bit less important. We have specifically chosen our own gauges where the yarns feel good and will shape into the finished forms we want. If your stitch gauge is a bit off, the piece will be somewhat smaller or larger. Everything is to be worn comfortably, so exact size is not imperative. However, when beginning a project or when trying out a yarn, you should always try to match the given stitch gauge. Be sure to knit a swatch and work towards achieving the goal of gauge. Throughout the designs, you will see that we have you knit to inch/centimeter measurements for stitches across and not to a specific number of rows. This way, row gauge is much less crucial and the ability to have a perfect fit will rely only on your ability to measure.

Making a Gauge Swatch

A good size swatch should be made over 4"/10cm worth of stitches. If you are working in a pattern stitch with a given multiple of stitches, you may have to make your swatch a bit bigger. Every pattern that we have written states a given gauge and tells you how many stitches to cast on for a 4"/10cm swatch. Here's an example:

12 sts to 4"/10cm over St st using MC and size 10½ (6.5mm) needles.

What this tells you is to cast on 12 stitches (3 stitches per inch) onto size 10½ (6.5mm) needles using the MC (main color) yarn. Work in St st (Stockinette stitch) for 4"/10cm.

Measuring a Swatch

The most accurate way to measure your gauge is to block your swatch first. To accomplish this, be sure the swatch is bound off, then place it flat on a dry surface with the wrong side facing up. Carefully hold a steam iron over the swatch, but do not let the iron physically touch it. Allow the steam to flow over the yarn, adding a bit of moisture. Run your hand over the swatch to uncurl all of the edges and even it out. Pin the edges down without stretching the swatch. Let it dry thoroughly, then unpin the edges, flip it over and take your gauge using a ruler or tape measure. We suggest measuring your gauge over the width of your swatch thus achieving an average by placing the ruler or tape measure horizontally across the center. This is the most accurate way to measure.

If your stitch gauge is off, adjust the needle size as necessary to come as close as possible. If you need more stitches per inch, take your needle size down one size at a time. If you need fewer stitches to the inch, take your needle size up one size at a time. When row gauge is required, you should measure vertically up the center.

If you find that you can get the stitch gauge but not row gauge, simply watch the number of rows worked and check the pattern schematics for the number of inches needed.

Saving Your Swatch

Making a swatch is not only a good test for getting the gauge, but for seeing how the yarn responds to blocking and cleaning. So, don't unravel the swatch, but keep it for future use.

Measuring Knitted Pieces

In order to keep things simple, we have given you measurements for all of the pieces that you will knit. If things come out a bit bigger or a bit longer, this will not really alter the finished look. We designed each of the styles for ease and comfort. However, we do have a special way to measure. For a long time, we used to measure our knitting flat and we found that everything came out too long. Gravity would take over once our pieces were held vertically. So we found it best to measure the knitting hanging down. To do this, knit following the instructions up to the specified measurement. Carefully spread your stitches out across the circular needle or two straight needles to distribute them evenly. Hold your knitting up and place a tape measure under the last rows of stitches and measure down vertically. If you are working a stitch pattern that requires a few rows more or less, work or don't work those rows.

Yarn Labels

These little pieces of paper are packed with loads if important information. Everything from the recommended needle size to gauge and from fiber content to cleaning directions. Not to mention how many ounces/grams and yards/meters there are per ball. Save a label from each of your projects for future reference; especially when it comes time to block or clean them.

Substituting Yarns

We know that everyone has personal likes and dislikes when it comes to colors and textures. To make life easier for you, we have given you "Design Options" at the end of many of the patterns. In some cases, we have given you yarn change ideas. Sometimes knitting the same design in a different yarn will give you a finished design that is completely different. A color change can also give you a whole new look.

If you are going to substitute a yarn, chose one that is similar in thickness to the one used in the project. The safest way of substituting is to look on the yarn label of the yarn called for in the directions to see the manufacturer's recommended needle size and gauge. Compare that label to the label of the yarn you want to use. Check to make sure the needle size and gauge match as closely as possible. When gauges match or are close, then you will have no problem getting the gauge called for in the pattern instructions. Here's a guide to better help you substitute one yarn for another.

Yarn Quantities

For each of the patterns in this book, we have written the quantity of balls of yarn to purchase. Along with this information, we have given you the number of yards/meters for each ball. If you are unable to find a specific yarn, please look for a yarn with similar texture (if that is what made you select this design) and the same thickness. To determine how many balls of the new yarn you'll need, get your calculator and work as follows:

Multiply the number of balls called for in the directions by the yards/meters stated. Let's say the directions state you'll need 10 balls and the yards/meters is 95 yards/87 meters per ball. Multiply 10 by 95/87 and you'll get 950 yards/870 meters. Divide this number by the yardage of the new yarn, say it's 82 yards/75 meters per ball. So, 950 yards/870 meters divided by 82 yards/75 meters gives you 11.5 /11.6 balls. Now round up to the next whole number. You'll need to buy 12 balls of the new yarn.

Since every dye lot of yarn will change the yards/meters in a ball, please watch the yarn quantity as you work a design. Once you have knit two or three balls, check to see how far they have taken you and see how much more needs to be knit. It is always best to purchase additional yarn while the dye lot is available. If you are not going to start a design immediately, you can work one ball of yarn to check for yardage or just simply purchase one or two extra balls of yarn. Most stores will allow you to return unused yarns as long as you retain your sales receipt, the yarn was not on sale, the yarn is returned within a given time period and the yarn is still current in that store. Please check with your retail store for their return policy.

You might find a yarn that you want to use, but the label lists only American or Metric yards/meters or ounces/grams information. You can use the yarn conversion chart, below, to convert measurements so you can calculate how many balls you'll need of the substitute yarn.

yards x .91 = meters
meters x 1.09 = yards
grams x .0352 = ounces
ounces x 28.35 = grams

Sizing Up Your Figure

Throughout Knitovation you will see that some of our designs are "one size fits all." We were able do this because of the types of yarns that we use create soft knitted fabrics that drape on the body, no matter what your body size. In some cases, we have written the patterns with sizes as the styles require a more specific fit. In each case, look at the finished bust measurements, both written out and on the schematics at the end of each pattern. We suggest that you forget the label of "small, medium and large." Instead, your only concern is that the finished size fits your body the way that you like.

In order to best judge what design features will work for you, you should look at yourself in the mirror. We know, you have just dropped this book and run from the room. Please be calm. It's important that everything fits and this is all that matters. So, look at yourself from your neck down to learn what body type you are.

Full busted—larger on top and narrow as you go down.
Straight body—shoulders, bust and hips are about the same width.
Hourglass—full busted, narrow waist and full hips.
Pear shaped—narrow shoulders, small bust and full hips.

Now you have to take some measurements. With the help of a good friend, use a tape measure to measure your bust around the fullest part. You may wish to take measurements of the upper and lower hips, but they will not be as important.

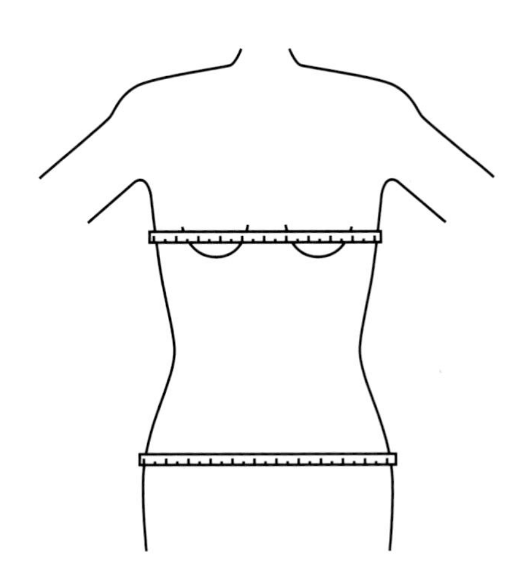

Once you have these measurements, think about the amount of ease you like in your sweaters and coats. If you are not sure, go through your wardrobe and try on some of your favorites and see how much ease they have in them and use their measurements as a guide for your preferred fit.

As mentioned, many of our patterns are "one size fits all." In every case, we show you what the finished measurements will be. We love that things fit easily around the body. If measurements are much too big and no size options appear, simply use needles that are a size or two smaller and the pieces will become proportionately smaller. This works in reverse so that if "one size fits all" is too small, simply go up a needle size or two and the finished piece will be larger. Always remember that we have designed these pieces for simplicity in knitting and ease in wearing. You should just relax and enjoy.

Butterflies Are Free

In many of the patterns, we used Hannah Silk ribbon for edgings and trims. This is a wonderful hand-dyed silk ribbon that is cut on the bias. We love to butterfly-tie this ribbon not only to remove the sewn seams, but to create an even more exciting trim. Whenever the pattern instructions says to butterfly-tie the ribbon, work as follows: unroll the ribbon from the spool until you reach a sewn bias seam. With sharp scissors, cut the bias seam off on each side and discard the seam.

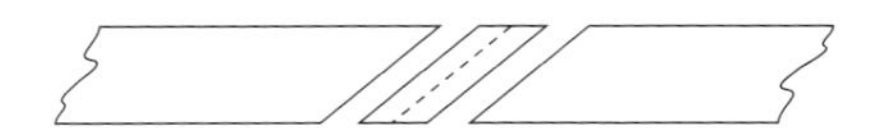

Continue to unroll the entire spool, removing the seams until all that remains are lots of strips. (If a ribbon is only going to be used around a neck edge, you can do a few yards/meters at a time instead of the whole spool.) To butterfly-tie, make a knot by placing the left-hand end over the right-hand end.

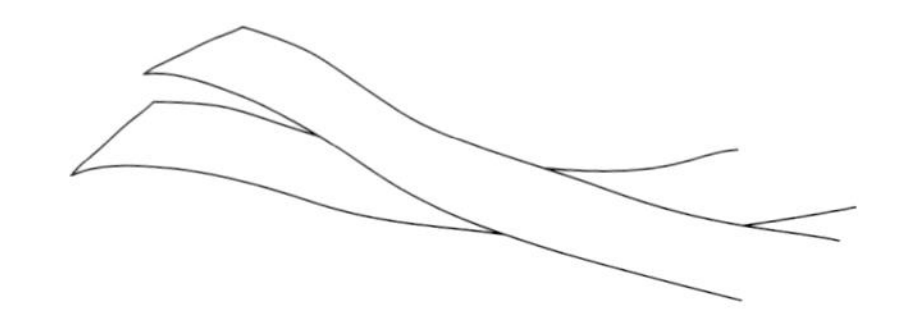

Now fold over both both ends of the pieces and tuck them through the resulting hole to create a loop.

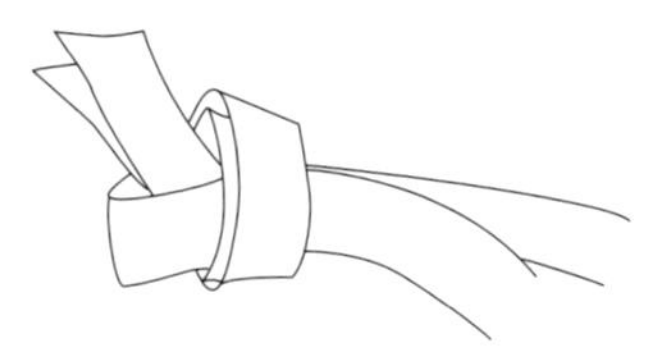

Pull on the ends to tighten and secure the knot. Trim the ends at an angle and so they are 2"/5cm long. Continue to knot strips together until you have one continuous strip. If the pattern calls for two or more colors, remove all the seams from all the spools and let the colors intermingle. Join the strips, picking colors at random, to create a unique colorway that is exclusively your own.

Supplies for Success

If you're anything like us, you purchase new needles for every project. Even though we are working on lots of projects all on the same size needles, we still have spare pairs. You never know when you get the itch to pick up a project, and this way you'll be prepared. We suggest that you keep a list of the needle sizes that you have. With each visit to a yarn store, you can fill in what you don't have...just in case. From our experience, we've found that every knitter has a favorite type of needle (circulars or straights) and a favorite type of material (wood or metal). If you are not sure, try them all to get a feel for what works best for you and your knitting style.

Along with needles, you should have a knitting bag or basket to hold all your little accessories. Don't you just love all those gadgets? Here is a list of some good items to have:

needle case holder
point protectors
knitting needle gauge
tape measure
row counter
stitch holders
stitch markers
sharp scissors
large eye yarn needle
blocking pins
note pad and pen

knitting terms/abbreviations

approx approximately

beg begin(ning)

CC contrasting color

ch chain(s)

cm centimeter(s)

cn cable needle

cont continu(e)(ing)

dec decrease(ing)

foll follow(s)(ing)

g gram(s)

garter stitch Knit every row.

inc increas(e)(ing)

k knit

k2tog Knit 2 stitches together

lp(s) loop(s)

m meter(s)

M1 make one stitch—With the needle tip, lift the strand between last stitch worked and next stitch on left-hand needle and knit into the back of it. One stitch has been added.

mm millimeter(s)

MC main color

oz ounce(s)

pat(s) pattern(s)

p purl

psso pass slip stitch(es) over

rem remain(s)(ing)

rep repeat

RS right side(s)

rnd(s) round(s)

sc single crochet (UK: dc-double crochet)

sk skip

SKP slip 1, knit 1, pass slip stitch over knit 1. One stitch has been decreased

sl slip—An unworked stitch made by passing a stitch from the left-hand needle to the right-hand needle as if to purl.

sl st slip st

ssk slip, slip, knit—Slip next 2 stitches knitwise, one at a time, to right-hand needle. Insert tip of left-hand needle into fronts of these stitches from left to right. Knit them together. One stitch has been decreased.

st(s) stitch(es)

St st Stockinette stitch—Knit right-side rows, purl wrong-side rows.

tbl through back loop(s)

tog together

WS wrong side(s)

wyib with yarn in back

wyif with yarn in front

yd yard(s)

yo yarn over-Make a new stitch by wrapping the yarn over the right-hand needle. (UK: yfwd, yon, yrn)

***** = Repeat directions following * as many times as indicated.

[ ] = Repeat directions inside brackets as many times as indicated.

Shoot from the hip. You'll win the West and everyplace else.

annie o

3 rectangles

three rectangles

annie o

SIZES

Instructions are written for size Small. Changes for sizes Medium and Large are in parentheses.

MATERIALS

Willow by Trendsetter Yarns, 1¾oz/50g balls, each approx 70yd/64m (polyester)

- 5 (6, 7) balls in #31 Black/Red (A)

Checkmate by Trendsetter Yarns, 1¾oz/50g balls, each approx 70yd/64m (polyamide/tactel nylon)

- 4 (5, 5) balls in #1037 Red/Blue/Gold (B)
- One pair size 15 (10mm) needles or size to obtain gauge
- Crochet hook size G/6 (4mm)
- Two Large hook and eye sets
- Matching sewing thread
- Sewing needle

GAUGE

9 sts to 4"/10cm over St st using 2 strands of A held tog and size 15 (10mm) needles.

9 sts to 4"/10cm over St st using B and size 15 (10mm) needles.

Take time to check gauge.

FINISHED MEASUREMENTS

Bust 36 (40, 44)"/91.5 (101.5, 111.5)cm

Length 20½ (21½, 22½)"/52 (54.5, 57)cm

NOTE

Work with 2 strands of A held tog throughout.

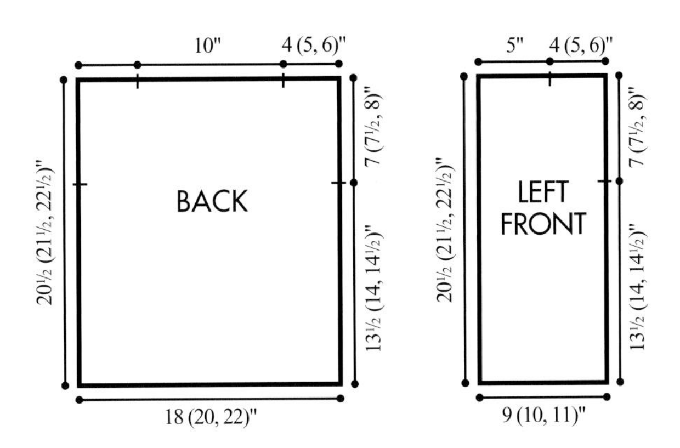

STOCKINETTE STITCH

Row 1 (RS) Knit.

Row 2 Purl.

Rep rows 1 and 2 for St st.

BACK

With with 2 strands of A held tog, cast on 42 (46, 50) sts. Work in St st for 4½"/11.5cm, end with a WS row. Cont in stripe pat as foll: *Change to B and work in St st for 3 ½ (4, 4½)"/9 (10, 11.5)cm, end with a RS row. Knit next row for garter stitch ridge. Change to 2 strands of A and work in St st for 4½"/11.5cm, end with a WS row; rep from * once more. Piece should measure 20½ (21½, 22½)"/52 (54.5, 57)cm from beg. Bind off.

FRONT (make 2)

With with 2 strands of A held tog, cast on 21 (23, 25) sts. Cont to work as for back.

FINISHING

Sew a 4 (5, 6)"/10 (12.5, 15)cm shoulder seam each side gathering fronts. Place markers 7 (7½, 8)"/17.5 (19, 20.5)cm down from shoulders. Sew side seams to markers.

Neck edging

From RS, join A with a sl st in top right front neck edge. **Row 1** Ch 1, making sure that work lies flat, sc evenly across neck edge to top left front neck edge. Do not ch, turn. **Row 2** Sl st in each st across. Fasten off.

Fringe

From a full ball of B, cut ribbon into checkerboard strands and suede ribbon strands. With RS facing and bottom edge of back at your right, insert hook, from right to left, under first st of first garter st ridge. Fold a checkerboard strand in half, then in half again. Draw center of strand through forming a loop. Pull ends of strands through this loop, then pull to tighten. Cont to make a fringe in every st of garter st ridge alternating suede strands and checkerboard strands. Rep for all ridges. Using needle and thread, sew on hook and eye sets at desired points on vest fronts to close.

DESIGN OPTIONS

- Make it a pullover by working two backs and assembling exactly the same leaving a neck opening.
- Make longer by working additional stripes.
- For a pear-shaped full figure, possibly work Willow at top area only. Or, make the vest a bit longer and leave 5"/12.5cm deep side vents to accommodate fuller hips.
- For a v-shaped full figure, check positioning of stripes and work an extra half-stripe to reposition Willow so it does not appear across the fullness of the bust. Be sure to keep overall length of the vest on the shorter side.

Wrap it up. Have your family and friends each knit a strip!

basketweave blues

12 rectangles

12 rectangles x twelve

basketweave blues

SIZES

Finished approx 56" x 70"/142.24 x 177.8cm.

Add additional strips in each direction. For a longer/wider throw.

MATERIALS

Crisantemo by Trendsetter Yarns, 1¾oz/50g balls, each approx 55yd/51m (polyester/viscose)

- 4 balls each in #15 Periwinkle (E) and #24 Lime Prime (A)
- 3 balls in #16 Olive (I)

Vintage by Trendsetter Yarns, 1¾oz/50g balls, each approx 95yd/87m (polyester/tactel nylon)

- 3 balls in #1039 Midnight Madness (D)

Dolcino by Trendsetter Yarns, 1¾oz/50g balls, each approx 100yd/92m (acrylic/polyamide)

- 4 balls in #30 Purple (B)

Coconut by Trendsetter Yarns, 1¾oz/50g balls, each approx 66yd/61m (polyamide)

- 4 balls in #12 Tahitian Tide (C)

Zucca by Trendsetter Yarns, 1¾oz/50g balls, each approx 71yd/65m (tactel/polyamide)

- 6 balls in #6079 Apple (F)

Spruce by Trendsetter Yarns, .87oz/25g balls, each approx 80yd/74m (acrylic/polyester)

- 3 balls in #8 Fatigues (G1)

Merino Otto by Lane Borgosesia/Trendsetter

Yarns, 1¾oz/50g balls, each approx 130yd/125m (wool)

- 4 balls in #27160 Dark Periwinkle (G2)

Voila Print by Trendsetter Yarns, 1¾oz/50g balls, each approx 180yd/165m (nylon)

- 1 ball in #21 Blue/Green/Purple (H)

Swing by Trendsetter Yarns, 1¾oz/50g balls, each approx 65yd/60m (polyamide/tactel nylon/lurex)

- 5 balls in #1841 Lime Green/Blues (J)

Aura by Trendsetter Yarns, 1¾oz/50g balls, each approx 148yd/135m (nylon)

- 1 ball in #9332 Navy (K)

Segue by Trendsetter Yarns, 3½oz/100g hanks, each approx 120yd/110m (nylon)

- 1 hank in #6 High Tide (L)
- One pair each sizes 8, 9, 10½, 11 (5, 5.5, 6.5 and 8mm) needles
- Crochet hook size F/5 (3.75mm)

GAUGE

Throw is made of 12 long scarf-style strips, of varying widths and lengths, that are woven together. Gauge is not important. The differences in gauges, yarn thicknesses and textures create the unique look and asymmetrical border.

FINISHED MEASUREMENTS

Approx 58"/147cm wide (at widest point) x 76"/193cm long (at longest point)

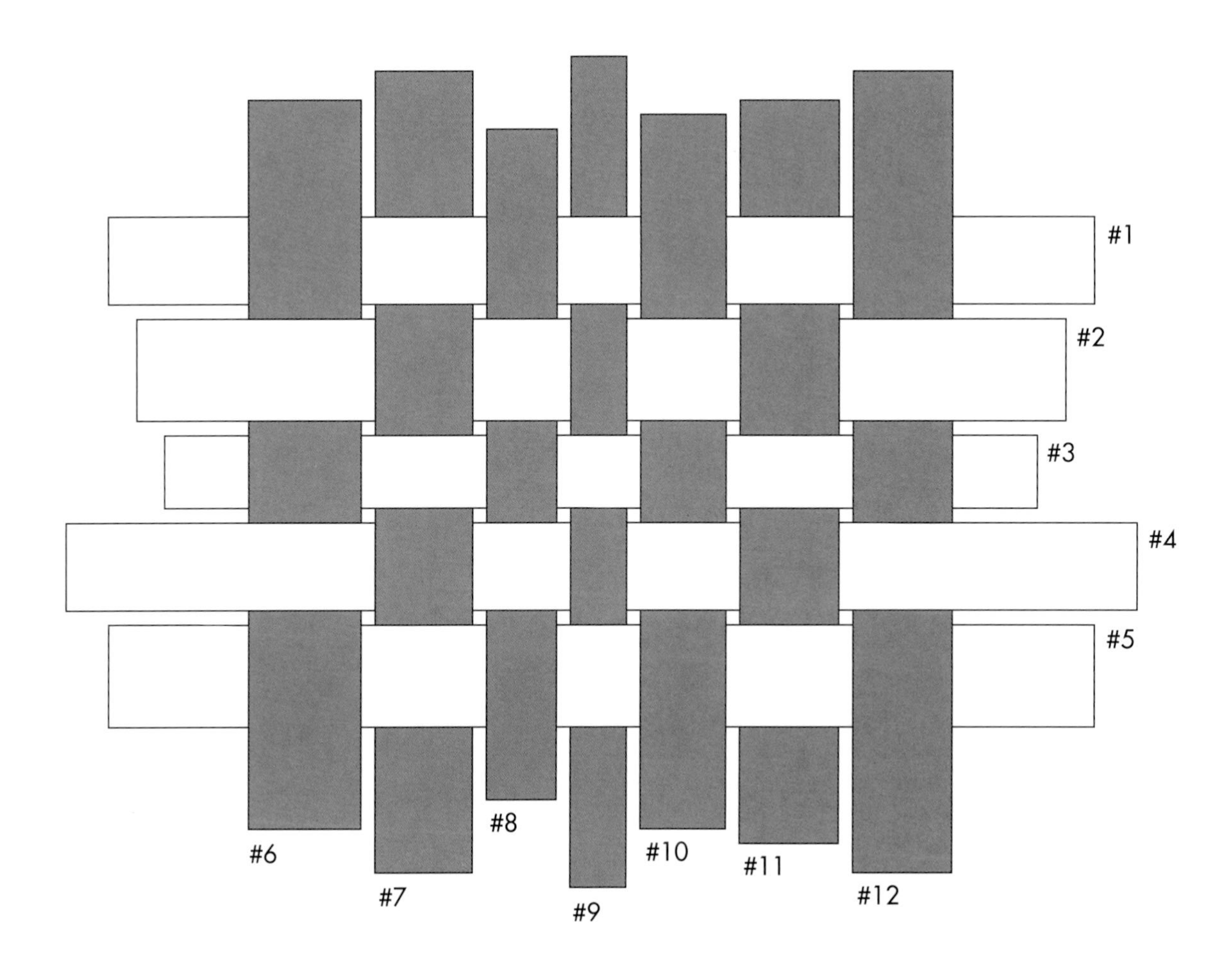

GARTER STITCH

Row 1 (RS) Knit.

Rep row 1 for garter st.

STRIP 1

With size 10½ needles and A, cast on 20 sts. Using all 4 balls of yarn, work in garter st until only enough yarn rem to bind off. Bind off.

STRIP 2

With size 10½ needles and B, cast on 24 sts. Using all 3 balls of yarn, work in garter st until only enough yarn rem to bind off. Bind off.

STRIP 3

With size 8 needles and C, cast on 24 sts. Using all 4 balls of yarn, work in garter st until only enough yarn rem to bind off. Bind off.

STRIP 4

With size 11 needles and D, cast on 24 sts. Work in garter st until 3½ balls have been used. Bind off.

STRIP 5

With size 11 needles and E, cast on 27 sts. Using all 4 balls of yarn, work in garter st until only enough yarn rem to bind off. Bind off.

STRIP 6

With size 11 needles and F, cast on 27 sts. Using 3 balls of yarn, work in garter st until only enough yarn rem to bind off. Bind off.

STRIP 7

With size 10½ needles and 1 strand each of G and H held tog, cast on 27 sts. Using all 3 balls of G and 2 balls of H, work in garter st until only enough yarn rem to bind off. Bind off.

STRIP 8

With size 10½ needles and 1 strand of H and I held tog, cast on 23 sts. Using 2 rem balls of G, work in garter st until only enough yarn rem to bind off. Bind off.

STRIP 9

With size 10½ needles and J, cast on 15 sts. Using 3 balls of yarn, work in garter st until only enough yarn rem to bind off. Bind off.

STRIP 10

With size 9 needles and K, cast on 25 sts. Using 3 balls of yarn, work in garter st until only enough yarn rem to bind off. Bind off.

STRIP 11

With size 11 needles and F, cast on 22 sts. Using rem 3 balls of yarn, work in garter st until only enough yarn rem to bind off. Bind off.

STRIP 12

With size 10½ needles and 1 strand each of K and L held tog, cast on 23 sts. Using 2 rem balls of K and entire ball of L, work in garter st until only enough yarn rem to bind off. Bind off.

FINISHING

Weaving

Make space on a large table. Referring to diagram, lay out strips 1-5 horizontally; as shown. Because they are all different lengths, take care to center them. Beg at the center, weave strip 9 vertically under and over the horizontal strips. Adjust the strip so the same amount extends above and below. Cont to weave strips from left to right, then front right to left. Step away from the throw and see that everything is woven evenly and each strip is centered.

Joining strips

Open the hank of M to form a ring. Cut through the hank at each end to make multiple strands. Thread 1 strand into a tapestry needle. At each intersection, insert needle through all layers of one corner, then bring needle up through all layers at adjacent corner. Knot ends securely leaving 2 tails. Cont to join strips tog in the same manner.

Chaining stitch tails

Make a slip knot close to base of a tail. Place slip knot on crochet hook. Work in ch st, fastening off when you come to the end. Rep for each tail.

DESIGN OPTIONS

- Buy extra yarns or use other yarns to fringe some of the ends to add extra length and extra detail.
- Work additional strips horizontally and vertically to make the throw even bigger.
- Make a matching pillow using a large knife-edge pillow in a color that matches the yarns. Purchase an extra ball of each yarn that you like best. Knit narrow strips, then weave them together to form the pillow front. Sew in place allowing ends to hang over pillow edge.

Knit up some fast, easy squares in fun Aran stitch patterns—you won't feel boxed in.

cubist

6 squares

cubist

MATERIALS

Merino Otto by Lane Borgosesia/Trendsetter Yarns, 1¾oz/50g balls, each approx 130yd/125m (wool)

- 12 balls in #25278 Olive
- One pair size 10 (6mm) needles or size to obtain gauge
- Cable needle (cn)
- Stitch markers
- 16" x 16" x 16"/40.5 x 40.5 x 40.5cm foam cube

GAUGE

18 sts to 4"/10cm over St st using size 10 (6mm) needles.

Take time to check gauge.

FINISHED MEASUREMENTS

16" x 16" x 16"/40.5 x 40.5 x 40.5cm

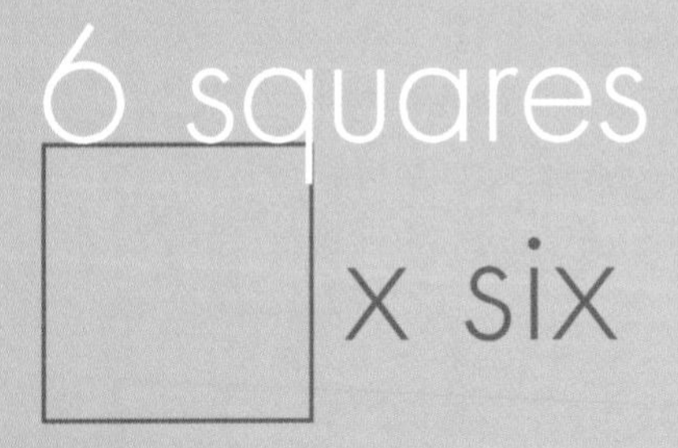

STITCH GLOSSARY

Bobble

[Yo, k1] 3 times in one st—6 sts. Turn work. Sl 1, p 5. Turn work. Sl 1, k5. Turn work. [P2tog] 3 times. Turn work. Sl 1, k2tog, psso—1 st.

TW2 (Twist 2 sts)

Knit second stitch on left-hand needle, knit first stitch on left-hand needle, slip both sts from needle tog.

BC (Back Cross)

Sl next st to cn and hold in back, k1 tbl, then p1 from cn.

FC (Front Cross)

Sl next st to cn and hold in front, p1, then k1 tbl from cn (Front Cross, FC), p4, k1.

6-st RC (6-st right cable)

Sl next 3 sts to cn and hold to back, k next 3 sts, k3 from cn.

6-st LC (6-st left cable)

Sl next 3 sts to cn and hold to front, k next 3 sts, k3 from cn.

STOCKINETTE STITCH

Row 1 (RS) Knit.

Row 2 Purl.

Rep rows 1 and 2 for St st.

HERRINGBONE SLIP STITCH PATTERN

(multiple of 4 sts plus 2 P/w2)

Row 1 (RS) K3, *sl 2 wyif, k2; rep from * to end K1.

Row 2 P2, *sl 2 wyib, p2; rep from *, end p2.

Row 3 K1, Sl 2 wyif, *k2, sl 2 wyif; rep from * to end K1.

Row 4 P4, *sl 2 wyib, p2; rep from *, end last rep p2.

Rows 5–12 Rep rows 1–4 twice more.

Row 13 Rep row 3.

Row 14 Rep row 2.

Row 15 Rep row 1.

Row 16 Rep row 4.

Row 17–24 Rep rows 13–16 twice more.

Rep rows 1–24 for herringbone slip st pat.

DIAMONDS AND BOBBLES

(multiple of 8 sts plus 1)

Row 1 (RS) K4, *p1, k7; rep from *, end p1, k4.

Row 2 P3, *k1, p1, k1, p5; rep from *,

end last rep p3.

Row 3 K2, *p1, k3; rep from *, end last rep p3.

Row 4 P1, *k1, p5, k1, p1; rep from * to end.

Row 5 *P1, k3, bobble in next st, k3; rep from *, end k1.

Row 6 Rep row 4.

Row 7 Rep row 3.

Row 8 Rep row 2.

Rep rows 1–8 for diamonds and bobbles pat.

CHECKERBOARD PATTERN

(multiple of 18 sts plus 12)

Rows 1, 3, 5, 7 and 9 (RS) K1, *[p1, TW2] 3 times, p1, k8; rep from *, end [p1, TW2] 3 times, p1, k1.

Rows 2, 4, 6, 8 and 10 K1, *[k1, p2] 3 times, k1, p8; rep from *, end [k1, p2] 3 times, k2.

Rows 11, 13, 15, 17 and 19 K1, p1, *k8, [p1, TW2] 3 times, p1; rep from *, end k8 tbl, p1, k1.

Rows 12, 14, 16, 18 and 20 K2, *p8, [k1, p2] 3 times, k1; rep from *, end p8 tbl, k2.

Rep rows 1–20 for checkerboard pat.

BOWKNOT STITCH

(multiple of 18 sts plus 9)

Row 1 (RS) K9, *p9, k9; rep from * to end.

Row 2 P9, *k9, p9; rep from * to end.

Rows 3 and 5 Knit.

Rows 4 and 6 Purl.

Rows 7 and 8 Rep rows 1 and 2.

Row 9 K13, *insert needle into front of next st 9 rows below and draw up a loop. Slip this loop onto left-hand needle and k it tog with next st, k17; rep from *, end last rep k13.

Row 10 Purl.

Row 11 P9, *k9, p9; rep from * to end.

Row 12 K9, *p9, k9; rep from * to end.

Rows 13 and 15 Knit.

Rows 14 and 16 Purl.

Rows 17 and 18 Rep rows 11 and 12.

Row 19 K4, *draw up a loop from 9 rows below and k it tog with next st, k17; rep from *, end last rep k4.

Row 20 Purl.

Rep rows 1–20 for bowknot st.

CHEVRON GARTER STITCH

(multiple of 11 sts)

Rows 1 to 5 Knit.

Row 6 (RS) *K2tog, k2, k into front and back of each of next 2 sts, k3, ssk; rep from * to end.

Rows 7, 9 and 11 Purl.

Rows 8, 10 and 12 Rep row 6.

Rep rows 1–12 for chevron garter st.

DIAMONDS WITH MOSS STITCH

(panel of 15 sts)

Row 1 (WS) P1, k5, p1, k1, p1, k5, p1.

Row 2 K1, p5, sl next 2 sts to cn and hold in front, k1 tbl, then sl the purl st from cn to left-hand needle and purl it, then k1 tbl from cn, p5, k1.

Row 3 Rep row 1.

Row 4 K1, p4, BC, k1, FC, p4, k1.

Row 5 and all foll WS rows Knit the k sts and purl the p sts.

Row 6 K1, p3, BC, k1, p1, k1, FC, p3, k1.

Row 8 K1, p2, BC, [k1, p1] twice, FC, p2, k1.

Row 10 K1, p1, BC, [k1, p1] 3 times, k1, FC, p1, k1.

Row 12 K1, BC, [k1, p1] 4 times, p1, BC, k1.

Row 14 K1, FC, [p1, k1] 4 times, p1, BC, k1.

Row 16 K1, p1, FC, [p1, k1] 3 times, p1, BC, p1, k1.

Row 18 K1, p2, FC, [p1, k1] twice, p1, BC, p2, k1.

Row 20 K1, p3, FC, p1, k1, p1, BC, p3, k1.

Row 22 K1, p4, FC, p1, BC, p4, k1.

Rep rows 1–22 for diamonds with moss st.

RIGHT TWIST CABLE

(panel of 10 sts)

Rows 1, 3 and 5 (WS) K2, p6, k2.

Row 2 P2, k6, p2.

Row 4 P2, 6-st RC, p2.

Row 6 Rep row 2.

Rep rows 1–6 for right twist cable.

LEFT TWIST CABLE

(panel of 10 sts)

Rows 1, 3 and 5 (WS) K2, p6, k2.

Row 2 P2, k6, p2.

Row 4 P2, 6-st LC, p2.

Row 6 Rep row 2.

Rep rows 1–6 for left twist cable.

SQUARE 1

Cast on 74 sts. Work in herringbone slip st pat until piece measures 16"/40.5cm from beg, end with a WS row. Bind off knitwise.

SQUARE 2

Cast on 65 sts. Work in diamonds and bobbles pat until piece measures 16"/40.5cm from beg, end with a WS row. Bind off knitwise.

SQUARE 3

Cast on 84 sts. Work in checkerboard pat until piece measures 16"/40.5cm from beg, end with a WS row. Bind off knitwise.

SQUARE 4

Cast on 63 sts. Work in St st for 4 rows. Cont in bowknot st until piece measures approx 15½"/39.5cm from beg, end with a WS row. Cont in St st for 4 rows. Bind off knitwise.

SQUARE 5

Cast on 66 sts. Work in chevron garter st until piece measures 16"/40.5cm from beg, end with a WS row. Bind off knitwise.

SQUARE 6

Cast on 90 sts. Set up pat sts as foll:

Next row (WS) Work row 1 of diamonds with moss st over first 15 sts, place st marker, work row 1 of right twist cable over next 10 sts, place st marker, work row 1 of diamonds with moss st over next 15 sts, place st marker, work row 1 of left twist cable over next 10 sts, place st marker, work row 1 of diamonds with moss st over next 15 sts, place st marker, work row 1 of right twist cable over next 10 sts, work row 1 of diamonds with moss st over last 15 sts.

For diamonds and moss st, work rows 2–22 once, then rows 1–22 3 times—88 rows. For both cable pats, work rows 2–6 once, then rows 1–6 13 times, then rows 1 and 2 twice—88 rows. Piece should measure 16"/40.5cm from beg, end with a WS row. Bind off knitwise.

FINISHING

Wet block all pieces to 16" x 16"/40.5 x 40.5cm. Let them dry. Sew side edges of squares 2, 3, 4 and 5 tog to form sides. Sew square 1 to top edges of sides to form top of cube. Sew one edge of last square 6 to form bottom. Insert foam cube. Sew rem side edges tog.

DESIGN OPTIONS

- You can use any stitch pattern that you desire. Just be sure to cast on enough stitches to form a 16" x 16"/40.5 x 40.5cm square. If you like only one pattern, you can just do that pattern. The choice is yours.
- To make the cube smaller, cast on less stitches, making sure to follow the appropriate multiple of stitches needed for each stitch pattern.

Treat yourself to something soft, cuddly, warm and luxurious.

blue lagoon

1 rectangle

blue lagoon

SIZE

One size fits all.

MATERIALS

Kashmir by Trendsetter Yarns, 1¾oz/50g balls, each approx 110yd/101m (cashmere/silk)

- 6 balls in #25275 Indigo (MC)

Fox Fur by Trendsetter Yarns, each ball approx 5yd/4.5m (fox fur/cotton)

- 1ball in Denim Blue (CC)
- One pair each sizes 7, 8, 9 and 10 (4.5, 5, 5.5, 6mm) needles or size to obtain gauge
- Crochet hook size H/8 (5mm)

GAUGE

18 sts to 4"/10cm over rib pat (slightly stretched) using MC and size 10 (6mm) needles.

Take time to check gauge.

FINISHED MEASUREMENTS

Bust 44"/111.5cm

Length 23"/58.5cm

Upper arm 23"/58.5cm

NOTE

Shrug is worked in one piece from sleeve edge to sleeve edge.

1 rectangle

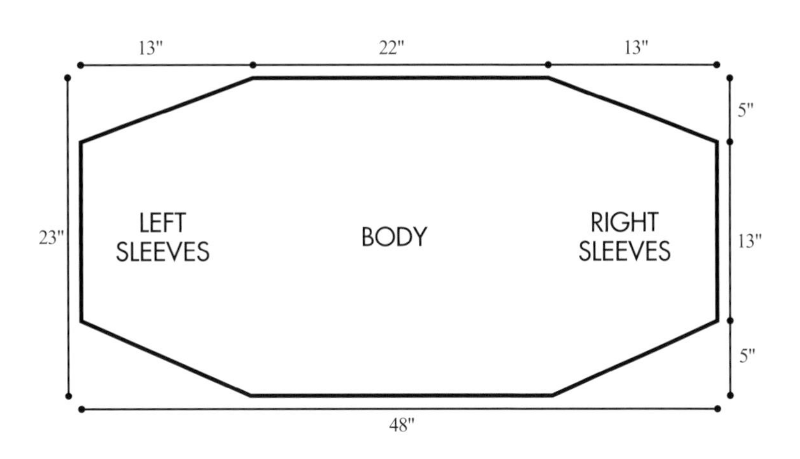

RIB PATTERN

Row 1 (RS) *K4, P4; rep from * to end. Rep row 1 for rib pat.

SHRUG

Right sleeve

With size 7 (4.5mm) needles and MC, cast on 104 sts. Work even in rib pat for 4"/10cm. Change to size 8 (5mm) needles and work in rib pat until piece measures 8"/20.5cm from beg. Change to size 9 (5.5mm) needles and cont in rib pat until piece measures 13"/33cm from beg. Mark beg and end of last row for end of right sleeve.

Body

Change to size 10 (6mm) needles and cont in rib pat until piece measures 22"/56cm from marked row.

Left sleeve

Mark beg and end of last row for beg of left sleeve. Change to size 9 (5.5mm) needles and cont in rib pat until piece measures 5"/12.5cm above last marked row. Change to size 8 (5mm) needles and cont in rib pat until piece measures 9"/23cm from last marked row. Change to size 7 (4.5mm) needles and cont in rib pat until piece measures 13"/33cm from last marked row. Piece should measure 48"/122cm from beg. Bind off in rib pat.

FINISHING

Sew sleeve seams to markers.

Upper edging

With CC, make a slip knot about 4"/10cm from a tuft of fur. Place slip knot on hook. Crochet a chain that measures same length as upper body edge from right underarm seam to left underarm seam. Fasten off. Using MC, sew in place.

Sleeve edging

With CC, make a slip knot about 10"/25.5cm from a tuft of fur. Place slip knot on hook. Crochet a chain that measures same length as bottom edge of sleeve. Fasten off. Using MC, sew in place.

DESIGN OPTIONS

- Leave piece unstitched, then fringe each end with Fox Fur to make a big wrap.
- Weave Fox Fur around all edges, then instead of sewing sleeve seams, sew medium size nylon snap sets on inside of Fox Fur. Snap sleeve seams closed for a shrug, or leave unsnapped for a big wrap.
- Omit Fox Fur and embellish with beads, flowers or ribbons.

What a sweet roll this tootsie is!

tootsie

1 rectangle

tootsie

MATERIALS

Surf by Prism Arts, 2oz/57g hanks, each approx 56yd/52m (nylon)

- 3 hanks in Nevada (MC)

Dover by Prism Arts, 2oz/57g hanks, each approx 150yd/137m (nylon/rayon)

- 2 hanks in Willow (A)

Hannah Silk bias cut ribbon, ⅝"/16mm-wide, each spool approx 40yd/36.5m (silk)

- 1 spool in Fresh Celery (B)
- One pair each sizes 10½ and 11 (6.5 and 8mm) needles or size to obtain gauge
- Size F/5 (3.75mm) crochet hook
- One large bag of polyester batting

GAUGE

16 sts to 4"/10cm over lace st using CC and size 10½ (6.5mm) needles.

12 sts to 4"/10cm over reverse St st using MC and size 11 (8mm) needles.

Take time to check gauge.

FINISHED MEASUREMENTS

7"/17.5cm-diameter x 18"/45.5cm long (not including ruffles)

1 rectangle

REVERSE STOCKINETTE STITCH

Row 1 (RS) Purl.

Row 2 Knit.

Rep rows 1 and 2 for reverse St st.

LACE STITCH

(multiple of 12 sts)

Row 1 (RS) *[K2tog] 3 times, [k1, yo,] 6 times, [k2tog] 3 times; rep from * to end.

Row 2 Purl.

Rows 3 and 4 Knit.

Rep rows 1–4 for lace st.

PILLOW

With size 10½ needles and A, cast on 72 sts. Work even in lace st for 8"/20.5cm, end on row 3. Change to size 11 needles and MC.

Next row (WS) K across, dec 18 sts evenly spaced—54 sts. Cont in reverse St st and work even until piece measures 30"/76cm from beg, end with a RS row. Change to size 10½ needles and A.

Next row (WS) P across, inc 18 sts evenly spaced—72 sts. Beg with row 1, work in lace st until piece measures 38"/96.5cm from beg. Bind off.

FINISHING

Sew long edge of MC section tog, leaving side edges of A sections unstitched.

Ruffle edging

From RS with crochet hook, join B with a sl st in seam. **Rnd 1** Ch 1, making sure that work lies flat, sc in evenly around entire edge of A section, working 2 sc in each corner. Join rnd with a sl st in first st. Fasten off. Cut B into 3"/7.5cm lengths. Tie butterfly bows (see page 11) along edging as shown or as desired. Cut batting into 18"/45.5cm wide strips. Roll into a tight pillow form that is 7"/17.5cm in diameter. Insert pillow form into pillow cover.

Ties (make 2)

With crochet hook and B, make a 20"/51cm long chain. Beg and ending at seam, weave each chain through row of eyelets closest to the MC section. Pull tight to gather in, then tie into a bow.

DESIGN OPTION

■ To make this bolster bigger or smaller, cast on more or less. Watch the number of stitches carefully as the lace stitch used for the ruffles has a big multiple. Change the pattern if necessary or work in garter stitch on big needles to allow fabric to really ruffle.

Cut ribbon and floral trim edges make *you* the material girl.

madonna

1 rectangle + 2 triangles

madonna

SIZES

Instructions are written for size Small. Changes for sizes Medium and Large are in parentheses.

MATERIALS

Tatiana by Lane Borgosesia/Trendsetter Yarns, 1¾oz/50g balls, each approx 110yd/101m (cotton)

- 2 (3, 3) balls in #245 Lilac (MC)

Segue by Trendsetter Yarns, 3½oz/100g hanks, each approx 120yd/110m (polyamide)

- 1 hank in #118 Moss and Lilacs (CC)

Flower Garden trim by Trendsetter Yarns

- 1 yd/1m in #118 Moss and Lilacs
- One pair size 5 (3.75mm) needles or size to obtain gauge
- Two size 5 (3.75mm) dpn for I-cord
- Crochet hook size G/6 (4mm)
- Matching sewing thread
- Sewing needle

GAUGE

20 sts and 26 rows to 4"/10cm over St st using MC and size 5 (3.75mm) needles.

Take time to check gauge.

FINISHED MEASUREMENTS

Bust 34 (36, 38)"/86.5 (91.5, 96.5)cm

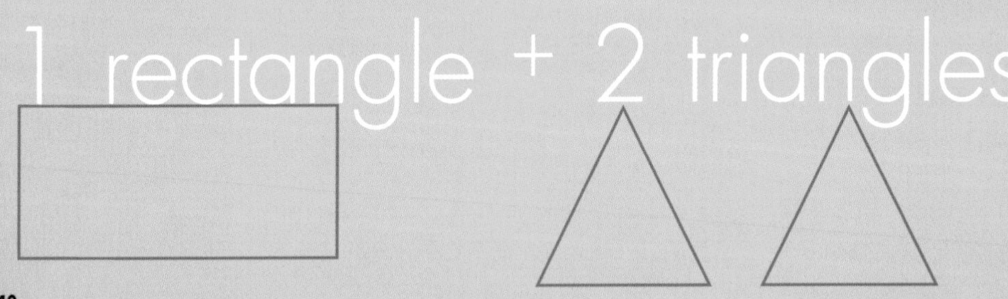

STOCKINETTE STITCH

Row 1 (RS) Knit.

Row 2 Purl.

Rep rows 1 and 2 for St st.

BOTTOM BAND AND BACK TIES

With MC, cast on 3 sts. Purl next row. Cont in St st and inc 1 st each end on next row, then every other row 4 times more—13 sts. Mark beg and end of last row. Cont in diagonal St st as foll:

Row 1 (RS) K1, k2tog tbl, k8, M1, k2.

Row 2 Purl. Rep these 2 rows until piece measures 44 (46, 48)"/111.5 (117, 122)cm above marked row, end with a WS row. Cont in St st and dec 1 st each end on next row, then every other row 4 times more—3 sts. Bind off.

CUPS (make 2)

With MC, cast on 41(45, 49) sts. Purl next row. Cont as foll:

Dec row (RS) K1, k2tog tbl, k to last 3 sts, k2tog, k1.

Next row Purl. Rep these 2 rows 17 (19, 21) times more—5 sts.

I-cord neck tie

Place rem 5 sts on dpn. Work in I-cord as foll: ***Next row (RS)** With 2nd dpn, k5, do not turn. Slide sts back to beg of needle to work next row from RS; rep from * until I-cord measures 28"/71cm from beg. Cut yarn leaving a long tail. Thread tail into tapestry needle and weave through sts. Pull tight to gather; fasten off securely.

FINISHING

Measure and mark center top edge of bottom band. With RS tog, position bottom edge of right cup on top edge of bottom band so RH bottom edge of cup overlaps center mark by 1"/2.5cm. Sew bottom edge of cup in place. With RS tog, position bottom edge of left cup on top edge of bottom band so LH bottom edge of cup overlaps center mark and right cup by 1"/2.5cm. Sew bottom edge of cup in place.

Neck edging

Mark center of Flower Garden trim. Pin center of trim to center vee between cups. Cont to pin trim along each neck edge, then each neck tie. Using needle and thread, sew trim in place.

Fringe

Along bottom edge of bottom band, measure and mark 1"/2.5cm from outside

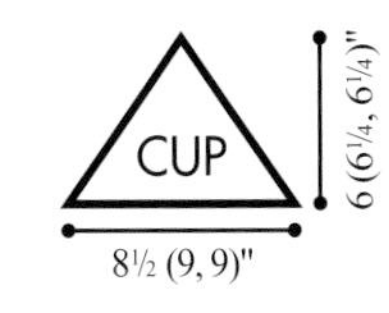

44 (46, 48)"

edge of each cup. You will be knotting fringe between these two marks. Cut CC into 20"/51cm strands. With RS facing and bottom edge of bottom band at your right, insert hook, from right to left, under the first inc (M1) st of diagonal St st at marker 1"/2.5cm from left cup. Fold one strand in half. Draw center of strand through forming a loop. Pull ends of strands through this loop, then pull to tighten. Cont to make a fringe in every other inc (M1) st to marker 1"/2.5cm from right cup.

DESIGN OPTION

■ If you'd like to add a bodice with a slit opening at the back, first try on the top before embellishing with trim or fringe. On bottom edge of bottom band, mark each side of the knot formed by the back ties. With RS of bottom band facing and Tatiana, pick up and k1 st in each st between markers. Beg with a purl row, continue in Stockinette stitch to desired length, end with a WS row. Change to Segue and bind off as foll: K2tog, *k2tog, bind off next st, k2tog; rep from * to end. Embellish as desired.

Her name is Lola and she is a showgirl...you will be too!

lola

3 rectangles

lola

SIZES

Instructions are written for size Small. Changes for sizes Medium and Large are in parentheses.

MATERIALS

Murano by Lane Borgosesia/Trendsetter Yarns, .87oz/25g balls, each approx 60yd/55m (nylon)

- 18 (20, 22) balls in #8 Sugar Plum (MC)

Hannah Silk bias cut ribbon, ⅝"/16mm-wide, each spool approx 40yd/37m (silk)

- 1 spool each in Her Majesty (A) and Cabernet (B)
- One pair size 8 (5mm) needles or size to obtain gauge
- Crochet hook size F/5 (3.75mm)
- Two stitch holders

GAUGE

17 sts to 4"/10cm over reverse St st using MC and size 8 (5mm) needles.

Take time to check gauge.

FINISHED MEASUREMENTS

Bust (closed) 46 (49, 52)"/117 (124.5, 132)cm

Length 23½ (25, 26½)"/59.5 (63.5, 67.5)cm

Upper arm 14 (15, 16)"/35.5 (38, 40.5)cm

NOTES

1) Body of jacket is made horizontally in one piece from left front edge to right front edge.

2) Back is more fitted than fronts. Fronts hang long to create the butterfly effect.

3 rectangles

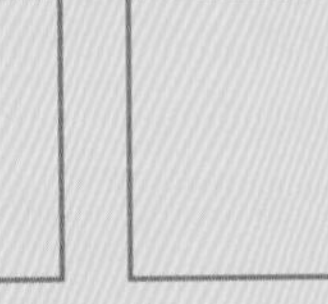

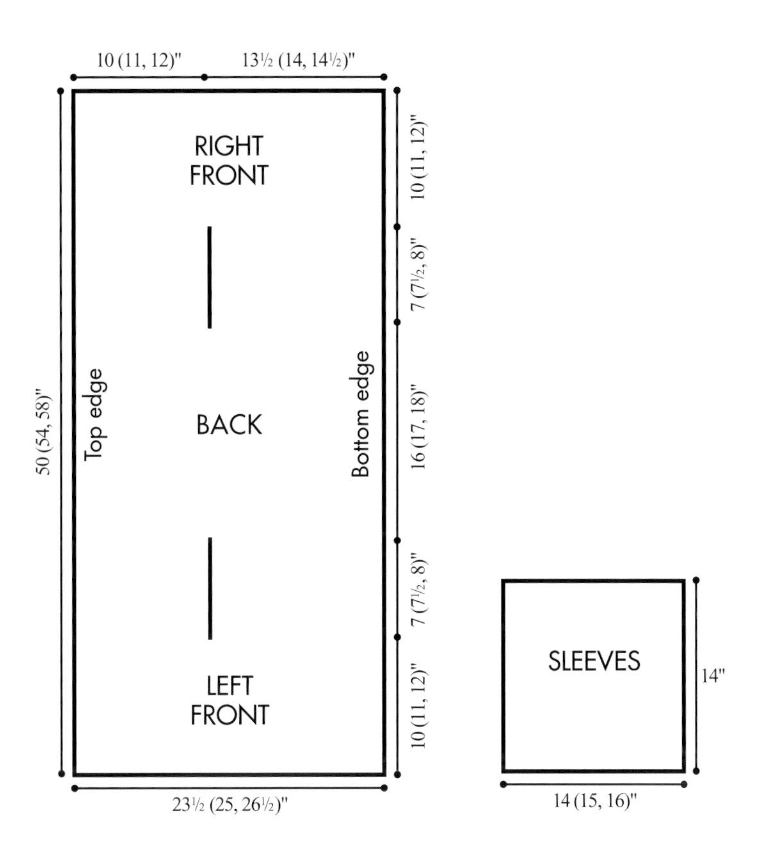

REVERSE STOCKINETTE STITCH

Row 1 (RS) Purl.

Row 2 Knit.

Rep rows 1 and 2 for reverse St st.

BODY

Beg at left front edge, with MC, cast on 100 (106, 112) sts. Work even in reverse St st until piece measures 10 (11, 12)"/25.5 (28, 30.5)cm from beg, end with a WS row.

Divide for left armhole

Next row (RS) P 58 (60, 62), join another ball of MC, p 42 (46, 50). Working both sides at once, work even until piece measures 17 (18½, 20)"/43 (47, 51)cm from beg, end with a WS row.

Next row (RS) P 100 (106, 112) sts, dropping 2nd ball of yarn. Join into one piece again for back. Work even until piece measures 33 (35½, 38)"/84 (90, 96.5)cm from beg, end with a WS row.

Divide for right armhole

Next row (RS) P 58 (60, 62), join another ball of MC, p 42 (46, 50). Working both sides at once, work even until piece measures 40 (43, 46)"/101.5 (109, 117)cm from beg, end with a WS row.

Next row (RS) P 100 (106, 112) sts, dropping 2nd ball of yarn to join into one piece again for rt. front. Work even until piece measures 50 (54, 58)"/127 (137, 147.5)cm from beg, end with a WS row. Bind off for right front edge.

SLEEVES

With MC, cast on 60 (64, 68) sts. Work even in reverse St st until piece measures 14"/35.5cm from beg. Place sts on a st holder.

FINISHING

Sleeve edging

Place sts from holder back on left-hand needle. Make a slip knot in end of A, then place slip knot onto crochet hook. **Row 1 (RS)** *Insert hook into next st on needle, yo and draw through ribbon, drop this st off of needle, yo and draw through both loops on hook, ch 1; rep from * across, insert hook into last st on needle, yo and draw through ribbon, drop this st off of needle, yo and draw through both loops on hook. Fasten off. Sew cast-on edge of each sleeve to armhole opening, making sure that underarm seam is centered on bottom edge of armhole. Sew sleeve seams.

Sleeve fringe

Cut A and B into 5"/12.5cm strands. Fold one strand of A in half. With WS facing, use crochet hook to draw center of strand through first st of sleeve edging, forming a loop. Pull ends of fringe through this loop. Pull to tighten. Cont to make a fringe in every 4th st of edging, alternating A and B. Butterfly-tie rem ribbons, alternating A and B (see page 11).

Outer edging

From RS, with crochet hook, join butterfly-tied ribbon with a sl st in center back neck edge. **Rnd 1** Ch 1, making sure that work lies flat, sc evenly around entire edge working 2 sc in each corner. Join rnd with a sl st in first sc. Fasten off. Pull all butterfly ties to RS.

DESIGN OPTIONS

- Jacket can be made longer by casting on additional stitches. Do not change position of armhole, just allow extra stitches to fall to bottom.
- Add a strand of Trendsetter's Eyelash to the main color yarn. This will bring a light look to the body and the flow of the design will allow the lashes to move.

Pick your favorite two fashion colors and go to town.

carla

5 rectangles

carla

SIZE

One size fits all.

FINISHED MEASUREMENTS

Circumference 18"/45.5cm

Length 10½"/26.5cm

MATERIALS

Voila by Trendsetter Yarns, 1¾oz/50g balls, each approx 180yd/165m (nylon)

- 2 balls each in #42 Aqua (A) and #1385 Burnt Orange (B)
- One pair size 5 (3.75mm) needles or size to obtain gauge

NOTE

Collar is reversible.

GAUGE

20 sts to 4"/10cm over St st using size 5 (3.75mm) needles.

Take time to check gauge.

5 rectangles x five

STOCKINETTE STITCH

Row 1 (RS) Knit.

Row 2 Purl.

Rep rows 1 and 2 for St st.

COLLAR

With A, cast on 90 sts loosely. Work in St st for 10½"/26.5cm, end with a WS row. Change to B and cont in St st until piece measures 21"/53cm from beg. Bind off loosely.

SCARF TIES

With a new ball of A, cast on 30 sts. Work in St st until only enough yarn rem to bind off. Bind off. Make another scarf tie using a new ball of B.

LOOP

With 2 strands of B held tog, cast on 20 sts. Work in St st for 5 rows. Bind off.

FINISHING

Sew back seam of collar forming a tube. With RS facing, insert B side inside A so bottom edges are even. Using A, loosely slip stitch bottom edges tog. Sew ends of loop tog, then sew to bottom back seam. Thread scarf ties through loop.

DESIGN OPTIONS

- Work the scarf ties in a stripe pattern.
- To add extra colors or textures, use a color coordinating Voila Print or another novelty yarn to make the ties.

Feel the music and dance to your heart's content...Olé!

carmen

2 triangles

carmen

SIZES

Instructions are written for size Small/Medium. Changes for size Medium/Large are in parentheses.

MATERIALS

Joy by Trendsetter Yarns, .87oz/25g balls, each approx 65yd/60m (polyamide/polyester)

- 10 (12) balls in #1339 Teal/Turquoise Tapestry (A)

Legacy by Trendsetter Yarns, 1¾oz/50g balls, each approx 60yd/55m (cotton/polyamide)

- 10 (12) balls in #7 ocean waters (B)
- Size 13 (8mm) circular needle, 36"/91.5cm longer size to obtain gauge

GAUGE

10 sts to 4"/10cm over garter st using A and B held tog and size 13 (8mm) circular needle.

Take time to check gauge.

FINISHED MEASUREMENTS

Width across top edge 52½ (55)"/133.5 (139.5)cm

Length to bottom point 26 (29)"/66 (73.5)cm

NOTES

1) Work with 1 strand each of A and B held tog throughout.

2) The circular needle is used to accommodate the large amount of sts.

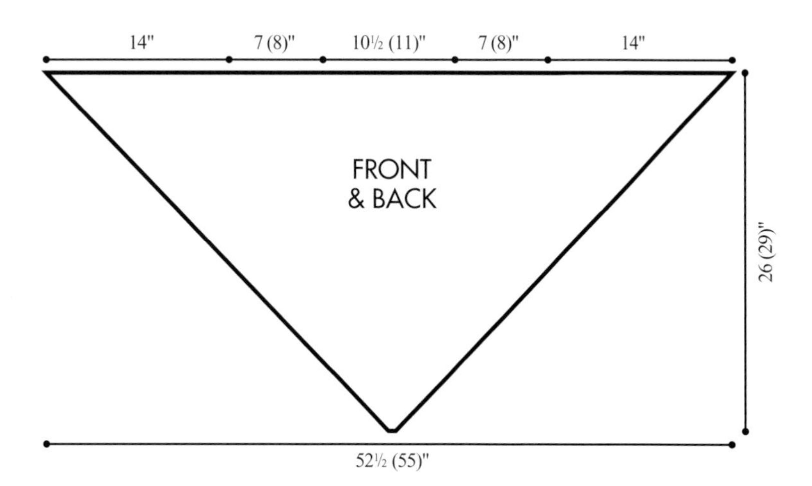

GARTER STITCH

Row 1 (RS) Knit.

Rep row 1 for garter st.

BACK

Beg at top edge, with A and B held tog, loosely cast on 131(137) sts. Do not join. Work back and forth in garter st, AT SAME TIME, dec 1 st each side on first row, then every other row 63 (14) times more, then every row 0 (52) times. Bind off 3 rem sts.

FRONT

Work as for back.

FINISHING

Working along top edge of back, measure and mark 14"/35.5cm in from each side edge. Measure and mark 7 (8)"/17.5 (20.5)cm in from each marker for shoulder seams. Repeat along top edge of front. Sew a 7 (8)"/17.5 (20.5)cm shoulder seam each side, leaving center 10½ (11)"/26.5 (28)cm open at center for neck opening. Slip piece on and tack front and back tog at side edges where desired.

DESIGN OPTIONS

- Both yarns selected have lots of lash and detail. If you prefer, select a flat yarn for either Joy or Legacy. Check to make sure you purchase enough balls of the flat yarn that equal the same yardage as the yarn you are substituting.
- Short tassels can be added to each top corner for additional embellishment.
- For a different fit to the body, sew a 14"/35.5cm seam each side, then just tack each side of neck opening. This will create cut out shoulders. If you wear something light, like a tube top, under the poncho, your bare shoulders will show and become part of the design.

Spread your wings and fly.

madame butterfly

3 rectangles

3 rectangles

madame butterfly

SIZES

Instructions are written for size Small. Changes for sizes Medium and Large are in parentheses.

MATERIALS

Mohair by Lane Borgosesia/Trendsetter Yarns, 1¾oz/50g balls, each approx 164yd/150m (mohair/Draylon acrylic)

- 8 (9, 10) balls in #7 Black (MC)

Maille by Lane Borgosesia/Trendsetter Yarns, .87oz/25g spools, each 300yd/275m (polyester/metal)

- 1 spool in Silver (CC)
- One pair each sizes 6, 7 and 8 (4, 4.5, 5mm) needles or size to obtain gauge
- Crochet hook size F/5 (3.75mm)

GAUGE

18 sts to 4"/10cm over reverse St st using MC and size 8 (5mm) needles.

Take time to check gauge.

FINISHED MEASUREMENTS

Bust (closed) 44 (45, 46)"/111.5 (114.5, 117)cm

Length 25 (27, 29)"/63.5 (68.5, 73.5)cm

Upper arm 16"/40.5cm

NOTES

1) Body of jacket is made horizontally in one piece from left front edge to right front edge.

2) Back is more fitted than fronts. Fronts hang long to create the butterfly effect.

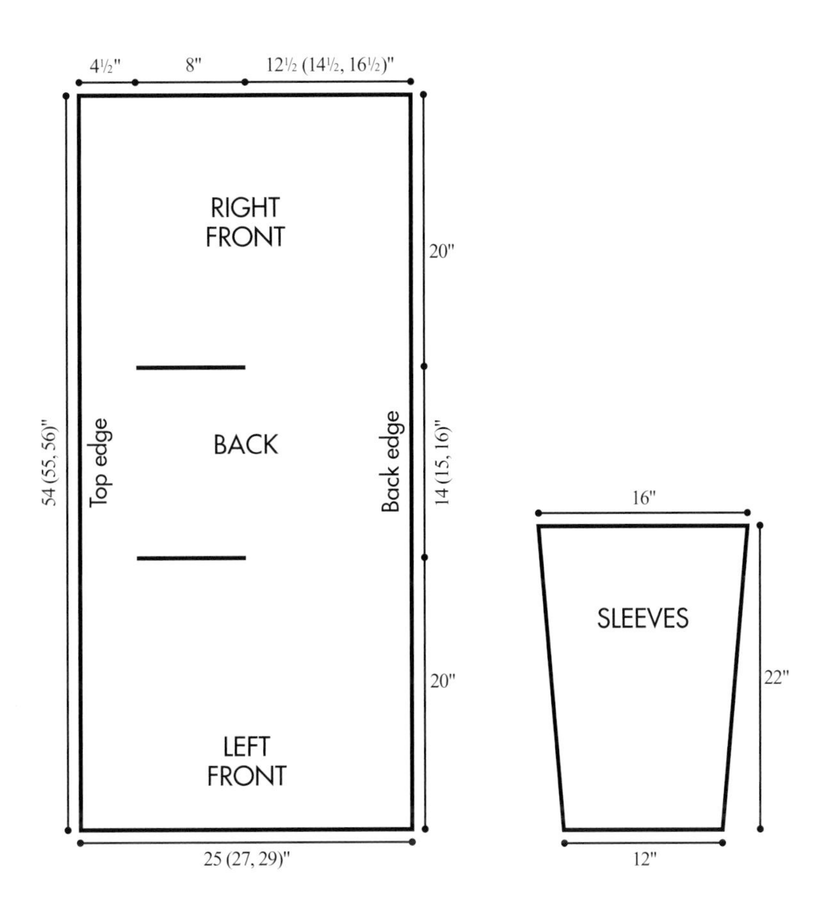

RIB PATTERN

Row 1 (RS) *K1, p1; rep from * to end.

Rep row 1 for rib pat.

REVERSE STOCKINETTE STITCH

Row 1 (RS) Purl.

Row 2 Knit.

Rep rows 1 and 2 for reverse St st.

BODY

Beg at left front edge, with size 8 (5mm) needles and MC, cast on 112 (122, 132) sts. Work in rib pat for 2 rows. Cont in reverse St st until piece measures 20"/51cm from beg, end with a WS row.

Left armhole

Next row (RS) P 56 (66, 76), bind off next 36 sts, p20.

Next row K20, cast on 36 sts, k 56 (66, 76). Work even until piece measures 34 (35, 36)"/86.5 (89, 91.5)cm from beg, end with a WS row.

Right armhole

Work as for left armhole. Work even until piece measures 54 (55, 56)"/137 (139.5, 142)cm from beg, end with a WS row. Cont in rib pat for 1 row. off in rib pat for right front edge.

SLEEVE

Beg at bottom edge, with size 6 (4mm) needles and MC, cast on 72 sts. Work in rib pat for 2 rows. Cont in reverse St st until piece measures 7"/17.5cm from beg. Change to size 7 (4.5mm) needles and work even until piece measures 14"/35.5cm from beg. Change to size 8 (5mm) needles and work even until piece measures 22"/56cm from beg, end with a WS row. Bind off.

FINISHING

Sew sleeve seams. Set sleeves into armholes making sure underarm seams are facing towards bottom edge of body.

Fringe

Cut CC into 11"/28cm strands. Fold one strand (as shown, or more as desired) in half. From RS, insert crochet hook horizontally through a st. Use hook to draw center of strand through, forming a loop. Pull ends of fringe through this loop. Pull to tighten. Cont to spread fringe around body as shown or as desired.

DESIGN OPTIONS

- Work both yarns together throughout for a complete tweed look. Be sure to buy extra metallic.
- You can frame all the pieces with a nice metallic edge as follows: cast on using Maille, then knit the next row. Change to Mohair and continue as directed. Before binding off, knit the last row using Maille, then bind off knitwise. For each armhole opening work as follows: with Mohair, p 56 (66, 76), change to Maille and bind off next 36 sts, join another ball of Mohair and p20. On the next row, k 20 using Mohair, then cast on 36 sts using Maille, work to end using Mohair. Drop Maille and 2nd ball of Mohair and continue as directed.
- Trendsetter's Dune can be substituted for this pattern. Leave off all the metallic fringe or replace Maille fringe with Hannah Silk ribbon fringe.

Knit two textured components in a drop stitch pattern. You're on Cruise Control.

cruise control

1 rectangle

1 rectangle

cruise control

SIZES

Instructions are written for size Small. Changes for sizes Medium, Large and X-Large are in parentheses.

MATERIALS

Charm by Trendsetter Yarns, .7oz/20g balls, each approx 94yd/86m (polyester/polyamide tactel)

- 7 (9, 11, 13) balls in #4207 Ocean & Sky (A)

Toreador by Lane Borgosesia/Trendsetter Yarns, .87oz/25g balls, each approx 198yd/180m (viscose/polyester)

- 3 (4, 5, 6) balls in #141 teal (B)

Hannah Silk bias cut ribbon, 7/16"/12mm-wide, each spool approx 40yd/37m (silk)

- 1 spool in Forrest Shed/Copper Patina (C)
- One pair size 9 (5.5mm) needles or size to obtain gauge
- Crochet hook size G/6 (4mm)

GAUGE

20 sts to 4"/10cm over St st using A and B held tog and size 9 (5.5mm) needles.

Take time to check gauge.

FINISHED MEASUREMENTS

Bust 54 (55, 55, 56)"/137 (139.5, 139.5, 142)cm

Length 18 (19½, 21, 22½)"/45.5 (49.5, 53.5, 57)cm

NOTES

1) Work with 1 strand each of A and B held tog throughout.

2) The vertical drop stitch pattern is created by unraveling stitches after knitting is completed.

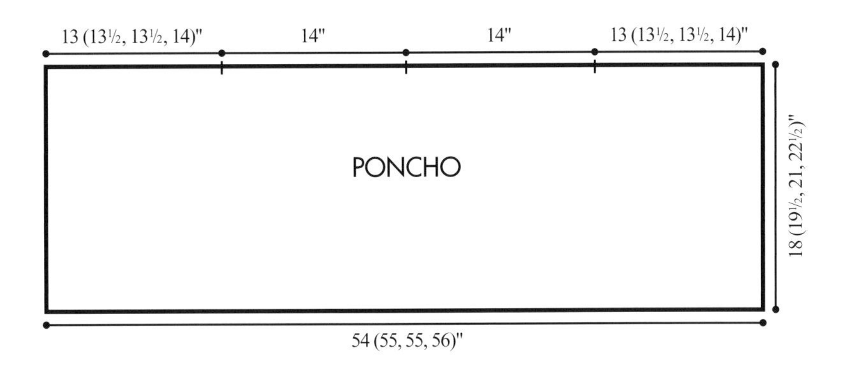

STOCKINETTE STITCH

Row 1 (RS) Knit.

Row 2 Purl.

Rep rows 1 and 2 for St st.

PONCHO

With A and B held tog, cast on 77 (83, 89, 95) sts.

Foundation row (RS) *K4, k2tog, yo; rep from * end k5. Beg with a purl row, cont in St st until piece measures 54 (55, 55, 56)"/137 (139.5, 139.5, 142)cm from beg, end with a WS row.

Last row (RS) *K5, drop next st off needle, yo; rep from *, end k5. Bind off evenly.

Unraveling stitches

Carefully unravel each dropped stitch down to yo of foundation row. Pull piece in each direction to open up the horizontal strands.

FINISHING

From WS, carefully steam-block piece following measurements; do not put steam iron directly onto knitting. Allow piece to dry. Fold piece in half lengthwise and sew a 13 (13½, 13½, 14)"/33 (34, 34, 35.5) shoulder seam, leaving a 14"/35.5cm wide neck opening. Butterfly-tie C (see page 11).

Neck edging

Position poncho so neck edge is at top and RS is facing you. Make a slip knot in end of C. Beg at shoulder seam, insert hook 1 st from top neck edge. On WS, place slip knot on hook and draw up to RS. Cont to work in slip st (see page 140) around entire neck edge, ending at beg shoulder seam. Fasten off. Push all butterfly ties to RS.

Outer edging

From RS, join C with a sl st in shoulder seam. **Rnd 1** Ch 1, *sc in each st to horizontal strand, ch 3, sk horizontal strand; rep from * to corner, work 2 sc in corner. Making sure that work lies flat, sc evenly across to next corner, work 2 sc in corner. Rep from * to * to next corner, work 2 sc in corner. Sc evenly across to next corner, work 2 sc in corner. Rep from * to * to shoulder. Join rnd with a sl st in first sc. Fasten off. Push all butterfly ties to RS.

DESIGN OPTIONS

- Make a simple shell using a solid color of Trendsetter's Sunshine, or another classic rayon yarn, to wear under this poncho to create a finished outfit.
- Run lengths of Hannah Silk ribbon through the horizontal strands of the unraveled stitches. Tie with bows at each end of work.
- Cut pieces of Hannah Silk ribbon, then tie into bows all over the poncho to embellish.

Make a few simple folds and you've got it.

origami

1 rectangle

origami

SIZE

One size fits all. Instructions are written for mid hip length. Changes for below hip length are in parentheses.

MATERIALS

Liberty by Trendsetter Yarns, 1¾oz/50g balls, each approx 65yd/60m (wool/nylon/acrylic)

- 8 (10) balls in #118 Moss and Lilacs (MC)

Segue by Trendsetter Yarns, 3½oz/100g hanks, each approx 120yd/110m (polyamide)

- 1 hank in #118 Moss and Lilacs (CC)
- One pair size 10½ (6.5mm) needles or size to obtain gauge
- Crochet hook size H/8 (5mm)

GAUGE

12 sts to 4"/10cm over St st using MC and size 10½ (6.5mm) needles.

Take time to check gauge.

FINISHED MEASUREMENTS

Bust (closed) 50"/127cm

Length 21 (23)"/53.5 (58.5)cm

NOTE

Body and sleeves are made horizontally in one piece.

1 rectangle

STOCKINETTE STITCH

Row 1 (RS) Knit.

Row 2 Purl.

Rep rows 1 and 2 for St st.

BODY AND SLEEVES

With MC, cast on 60sts. Work in St st until piece measures 60 (64)"/152.5 (162.5)cm from beg. Bind off.

FINISHING

Referring to diagram I, fold piece in half, cast-on and bound-off edges even. Sew back seam (from A to B) for 7"/17.5cm, leaving 13"/33cm unstitched for back bottom vent. Referring to diagram II, position back seam along center. Sew rem back seam (from A to B) for 14"/35.5cm, leaving 8 (9)"/20.5 (23)cm unstitched each side for sleeve openings.

Outer edging

From RS with crochet hook, join CC with a sl st in top edge of back bottom vent.

Rnd 1 Ch 1, working from left to right, and making sure that work lies flat, reverse sc evenly around entire outer edge. Join rnd with a sl st in first sc. Fasten off. Try on jacket. Fold neck edge over to desired width for collar, then tack edge in place at center back.

DESIGN OPTIONS

- If changing yarns, be sure to choose one that has some firmness, but also drapes nicely like Liberty.
- The jacket can be made even longer to create a car coat style by adding an additional 12 sts. Always be sure to check the gauge before your begin to work.
- For a fun alternative, work in stripes of St st and garter st to elongate the look of the body. Alternate stripe widths for even more interest.

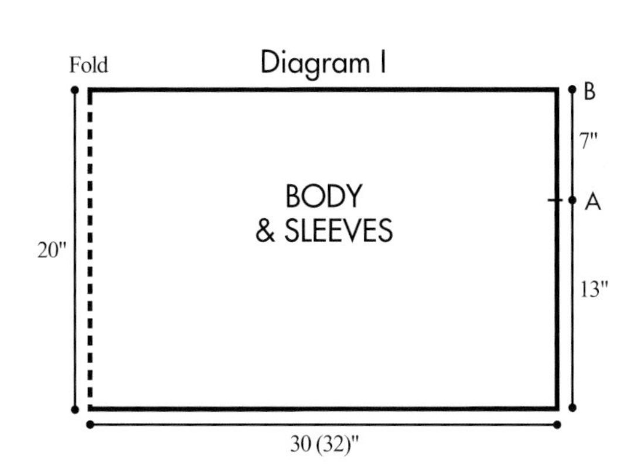

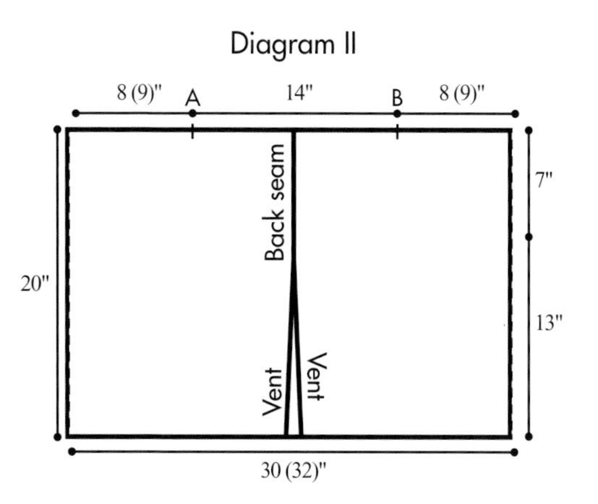

Sweet & delicious in more than 31 flavors.

gelato

3 squares

gelato

SIZES

Instructions are written for size Petite/Small. Changes for size Medium/Large is in parentheses.

MATERIALS

Crisantemo by Trendsetter Yarns, 1¾oz/50g balls, each approx 55yd/110m (polyester/viscose/ polyamide)

- 6 (7) balls in #27 Mandarin Madness (A)

Joy by Trendsetter Yarns, .87oz/25g balls, each approx 65yd/60m (polyamide/polyester)

- 6 (7) balls in #1194 Spring (B)

Hannah Silk bias cut ribbon, ⅝"/16mm-wide, each spool approx 40yd/37m (silk)

- 1 spool in California Poppy (C)
- One pair size 17 (12.75mm) needles or size to obtain gauge
- Size J/10 (6mm) crochet hook

GAUGE

8 sts to 4"/10cm over St st using A and B held tog and size 17 (12.75mm) needles.

Take time to check gauge.

FINISHED MEASUREMENTS

Bust (closed) 38 (42)"/96.5 (106.5)cm

Length 16 (17)"/40.5 (43)cm

NOTES

1) Work with 1 strand each of A and B held tog throughout.

2) Jacket is made of squares turned on end and folded.

3) All three squares must measure exactly 16" x 16" (17" x 17")/40.5cm x 40.5cm (43cm x 43cm) so that all seams match up.

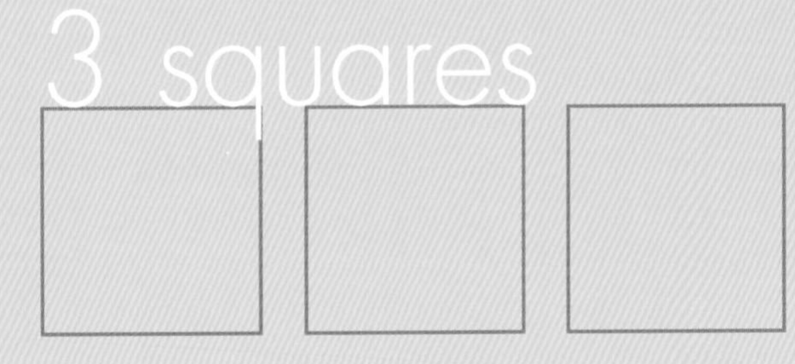

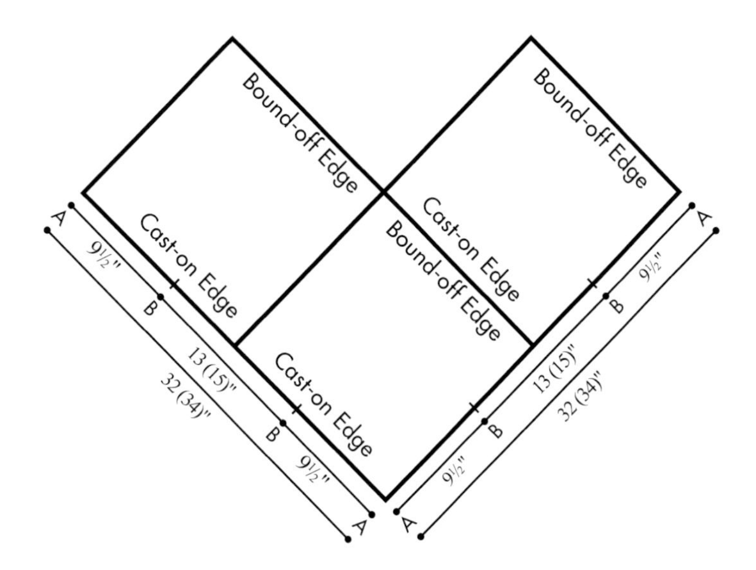

STOCKINETTE STITCH

Row 1 (RS) Knit.

Row 2 Purl.

Rep rows 1 and 2 for St st.

SQUARES (make 3)

With A and B held tog, cast on 32 (34) sts loosely and evenly. Work in St st until piece measures 16 (17)"/40.5 (43)cm from beg. Bind off.

FINISHING

Sew squares tog foll diagram. Along right-hand edge, fold squares in half along seam, matching As and Bs. Sew 9½"/23cm side seam (from A to B) leaving a 13 (15)"/33 (38)cm armhole opening. Rep along left-hand edge. Butterfly-tie C (see page 11).

Outer edging

From RS, join C with a sl st in back neck seam. **Rnd 1** Ch 1, making sure that work lies flat, sc evenly around entire edge, working 2 sc in each corner. Join rnd with a sl st in first sc. **Rnd 2** Working on the foundation of sc sts, work slip st (see page 140) in each st around. Fasten off. Pull all butterfly ties to RS.

DESIGN OPTIONS

- You can make this jacket bigger by making bigger squares. Keep in mind that the bigger the squares, the longer the finished piece. Watch carefully as you work to make sure the three pieces are all the same size and perfectly square.
- If substituting yarn, watch gauge carefully. It is best to work with yarns that will have some ease and some give as this design needs to move easily around the body.

This hat & gloves set will make you feel like the *real* First Lady.

jackie oooh

4 rectangles + 1 square

jackie oooh

SIZE

One size fits all.

MATERIALS

Dune by Trendsetter Yarns, 1¾oz/50g balls, each approx 90yd/83m (mohair/acrylic/viscose/nylon/metal)

- 3 balls in #61 Bright Primaries (MC)

Bunny by Trendsetter Yarns, each ball approx 10yd/9.5m (rabbit)

- 1 ball in Red (CC)
- One pair size 9 (5.5mm) needles or size to obtain gauge
- Crochet hook size H/8 (5mm)
- Large pillbox hat form

GAUGE

16 sts to 4"/10cm over rib pat using MC and size 10 (6mm) needles.

Take time to check gauge.

FINISHED MEASUREMENTS

Hat

Circumference 20½"/52cm

RIB PATTERN

Row 1 (RS) *K2, p2; rep from * to end.

Rep row 1 for rib pat.

SEED STITCH

Row 1 *K1, p1; rep from * to end.

Row 2 Knit the p sts and purl the k sts.

Rep row 2 for seed st.

REVERSE STOCKINETTE STITCH

Row 1 (RS) Purl.

Row 2 Knit.

Rep rows 1 and 2 for reverse St st.

HAT BRIM

With MC, cast on 16 sts. Work even in rib pat until piece measures same length as circumference of hat form. Bind off in rib pat.

CROWN

With MC, cast on 33 sts. Work even in seed st until piece measures 8½"/21.5cm from beg. Bind off in seed st.

FINISHING

Sew short edges of brim tog. Place brim around hat form brim, placing seam at center back. Sew top edge of brim to top edge of hat form. (Note the first 6 sts along bottom edge of brim will extend beyond the bottom edge of the hat form brim.) Place crown on hat form crown, positioning one corner at center back, opposite corner at center front, and the two rem corners at right and left. On RS of center back, bring the point of the corner over the knitted brim so the tip is even with bottom edge of hat form (underneath the 6 sts of the knitted brim). Tack in place. Rep for center front of crown, then for 2 rem corners. Working in running stitch, sew entire edge of crown to hat form.

Flower

With MC, cast on 80 sts leaving a 12"/30.5cm tail. Work St st for 1½". Bind off. Thread tail into tapestry needle. Sew a running st along cast-on edge. Pull tight to gather edge, then wind edge in concentric circles to form flower. Sew through all layers to secure flower tog.

Flower center

With CC and crochet hook, ch 3. Fasten off. Sew to center of flower, then sew flower to center front of hat.

GLOVES (make 2)

Beg at hand edge with smaller needles, cast on 32 sts. Work in rib pat for 2"/5cm. Mark beg and end of last row for beg of thumb opening. Work even for 2"/5cm. Mark beg and end of last row for end of thumb opening. Cont to work even until piece measures 9"/23cm from beg. Bind off in rib pat using larger needles.

FINISHING

Edging

From RS, with crochet hook, join CC with a sl st in first st of cast-on edge. **Row 1 (RS)** Ch 1, making sure that work lies flat, sc evenly across. Fasten off. For each glove, sew side seam leaving thumb opening unstitched.

DESIGN OPTIONS

- Use a long lash yarn such as Trendsetter's Crisantemo instead of Bunny.
- Sew additional Bunny or long lash yarn to edge of crown to make a furry border.

This Wild Stuff might just unleash your alter ego.

diva

5 rectangles

diva

MATERIALS

Wild Stuff by Prism Arts, 6.8oz/194g full hanks, each approx 300yd/275m and 3,4oz/97g half hanks, each approx 150yd/137m (wool/ mohair/cotton/rayon/nylon/polyester/silk)

- 2 (3, 3) whole hanks and 1 (0, 1) half hank in Captiva (MC)

Voila by Trendsetter Yarns, 1¾oz/50g balls, each approx 180yd/165m (nylon)

- 1 ball in #8283 Yellow (CC)
- One pair size 9 (5,5mm) needles or size to obtain gauge
- Crochet hook size G/6 (4mm)

GAUGE

18 sts to 4"/10cm over garter st using MC and size 9 (5.5mm) needles.

Take time to check gauge.

FINISHED MEASUREMENTS

Bust (closed) 38 (42, 46)"/96.5 (106.5, 117)cm

Length 22"/56cm

Upper arm 14 (15, 15)"/35.5 (38, 38)cm

NOTES

1) Wild Stuff (MC) consists of multiple hand-dyed fibers that are tied together. The tails are a design component of the yarn. Pull some or all of the tails to the RS to become part of the excitement of this jacket.

2) Work with 2 strands of CC held tog.

5 rectangles x five

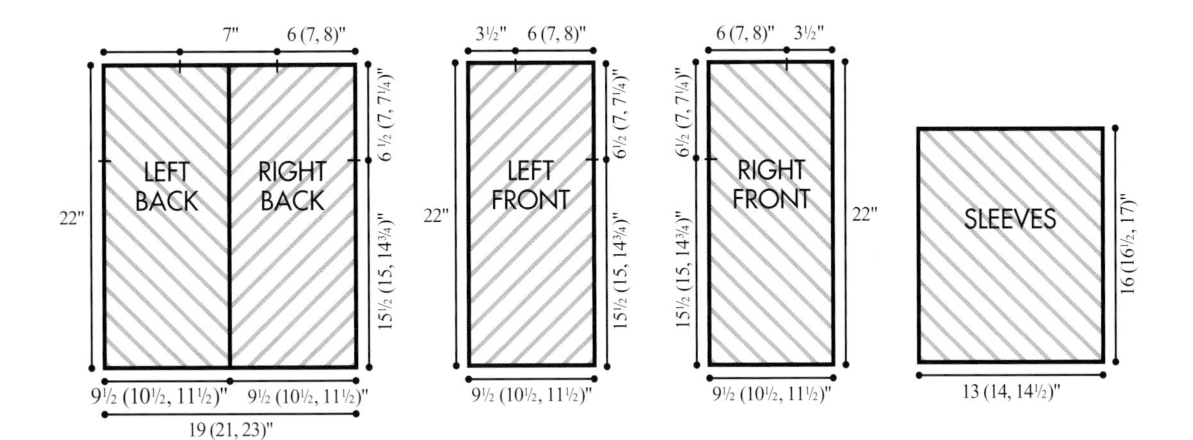

STITCH GLOSSARY

M1 (make one)

With tip of the needle, lift strand from the front between last stitch knitted and next stitch on left-hand needle. Place strand on left-hand needle, then knit into back of it to increase one stitch.

GARTER STITCH

Row 1 (RS) Knit.

Rep row 1 for garter st.

RIGHT BACK

With MC, cast on 3 sts. Knit first row.

Cont in diagonal garter st and inc as foll:

Inc row 1 (RS) K1, M1, k1, M1, k1.

Next row Knit.

Inc row 2 K1, M1, k to before last st, M1, k1.

Next row Knit. Rep last 2 rows until side edge of triangle measures 9½ (10½, 11½)"/24 (26.5, 29)cm, end with a WS row. Cont in garter st and maintain width of piece as foll:

Next row (RS) K1, M1 k to within 3 sts of end, k2tog, k1.

Next row Knit. Rep last 2 rows until the long side edge measures 22"/56cm from beg. Cont in garter st and dec as foll:

Dec row (RS) K1, k2tog tbl, k to last 3 sts, k2tog, k1.

Next row Knit. Rep last 2 rows until 3 sts rem. Bind off.

LEFT BACK

With MC, cast on 3 sts. Knit first row.

Cont in diagonal garter st and inc as foll:

Inc row 1 (RS) K1, M1, k1, M1, k1.

Next row Knit.

Inc row 2 K1, M1, k to with last st, M1, k1.

Next row Knit. Rep last 2 rows until side edge of triangle measures 9½ (10½, 11½)"/24 (26.5, 29)cm, end with a WS row. Cont in garter st and maintain width of piece as foll:

Next row (RS) K1, k2tog tb1, k to within last st, M1 k1.

Next row Knit. Rep last 2 rows until the long side edge of the piece measures 22"/56cm from beg. Cont in garter st and dec as foll:

Dec row (RS) K1, k2tog tbl, k to last 3 sts, k2tog tbl, k1.

Next row Knit. Rep last 2 rows until 3 sts rem. Bind off.

LEFT FRONT

Work as for right back.

RIGHT FRONT

Work as for left back.

SLEEVES

With MC, cast on 3 sts. Knit first row.

Cont in diagonal garter st and inc as foll:

Inc row 1 (RS) K1, M1, k1, M1, k1.

Next row Knit.

Inc row 2 K1, M1, k to with last st, M1, k1.

Next row Knit. Rep last 2 rows until side edge of triangle measures is 13 (14, 14½)"/35.5 (38, 38)cm, end with a WS row. Cont in garter st and maintain width of piece as foll:

Next row (RS) K1, M1, k to within last 3 sts, k2tog tbl, k1.

Next row Knit. Rep last 2 rows until the long side edge of the piece measures 16 (16½, 17)"/43 (44.4, 45.5)cm from beg. Cont in garter st and dec as foll:

Dec row (RS) K1, k2tog tbl, k to last 3 sts, k2tog tbl, k1.

Next row Knit. Rep last 2 rows until 3 sts rem. Bind off.

FINISHING

Sew side edges of back panels tog to create upward or downward chevron. Sew a 6 (7, 8)"/15 (17.5, 20.5)cm shoulder seam each side. Place markers 7 (7½, 7½)"/17.5 (19, 19)cm down from shoulders. Sew sleeves to armholes between markers. Sew side seams to within 7"/17.5cm of bottom edge for side vents.

Sew sleeve seams to within 3"/7.5cm of bottom edge for underarm vents.

Outer edging

From RS with crochet hook and 2 strands of CC held tog, join yarn with a sl st in base of any side vent. Rnd 1 Ch 1, making sure that work lies flat, sc evenly around entire edge, working 2 sc in each corner. Join rnd with a sl st in first sc. Fasten off.

Sleeve edging

From RS with crochet hook and 2 strands of CC held tog, join yarn with a sl st in underarm seam. Cont to work as for outer edging. Fold back each cuff 3"/7.5cm and tack at underarm seam.

DESIGN OPTIONS

- Lay out pieces on your work surface before sewing together to decide on whether or not you want the chevron pattern. Maybe pin the pieces together and hold up to see how it looks on the body.
- Find a ribbon like Trendsetter's Segue, ⅝"/16mm-wide Hannah Silk or Prism's Rococo and cut pieces of different lengths. Tie lengths around each of the yarn ties from Wild Stuff to decorate the jacket even more.
- Make a matching shell to go under the jacket using the same ribbon as the ties to create and exquisite suit.

East meets West in this American beauty.

shanghai

3 rectangles

shanghai

SIZES

Instructions are written for size Small/Medium. Changes for size Large/X-Large is in parentheses.

MATERIALS

Voila by Trendsetter Yarns, 1¾oz/50g balls, each approx 180yd/165m (nylon)

- 6 (7) balls in #26 Blue (MC)

Voila Print by Trendsetter Yarns, 1¾oz/50g balls, each approx 180yd/165m (nylon)

- 2 balls in #26 Blue/Green/Brown (CC)
- One pair size 5 (3.75mm) needles or size to obtain gauge
- Size G/6 (4mm) crochet hook

GAUGE

20 sts to 4"/10cm over St st using size 5 (3.75mm) needles.

Take time to check gauge.

FINISHED MEASUREMENTS

Bust (closed) 64 (68)"/162.5 (172.5)cm

Length 26"/66cm

Upperarm 26"/66cm

3 rectangles

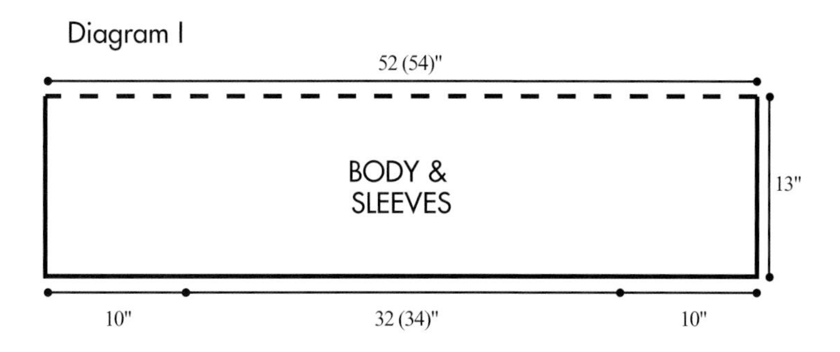

REVERSE STOCKINETTE STITCH

Row 1 (RS) Purl.

Row 2 Knit.

Rep rows 1 and 2 for reverse St st.

STOCKINETTE STITCH

Row 1 (RS) Knit.

Row 2 Purl.

Rep rows 1 and 2 for St st.

BODY AND SLEEVES (make 2)

With MC, cast on 80 (90) sts. Work even in St st until piece measures 26"/66cm from beg. Bind off.

COLLAR AND TIES

With CC, cast on 48 sts. Work in St st until piece measures 66"/167.5cm from beg. Bind off.

FINISHING

Sew short edges of body/sleeves tog forming a 52"/132 (137)cm long strip. Referring to diagram I, fold strip in half. Sew each underarm seam (from A to B) for 10"/25.5cm. Referring to diagram II, position underarm seams along center. Sew each side seam (from A to B) for 5½ (5)"/14 (12.5)cm, leaving 7½ (8)"/19 (20.5)cm unstitched for sleeve opening. Fold collar/ties piece in length lengthwise, WS facing. Sew edges tog leaving a 20"/51cm opening along center of side edge. Turn to RS; sew opening closed. Place center of collar/ties at center of back neck edge. Sew seam edge of collar/ties to neck edge to within 1"/2.5cm of each underarm seam.

Sleeve edging

From RS with crochet hook, join CC with a sl st in underarm seam. **Rnd 1** Ch 1, making sure that work lies flat, sc in evenly around. Join rnd with a sl st in first st. Fasten off.

DESIGN OPTIONS

- Work body and sleeves in single rib to add more texture.
- Stripe body and sleeves using Voila and Voila Print.

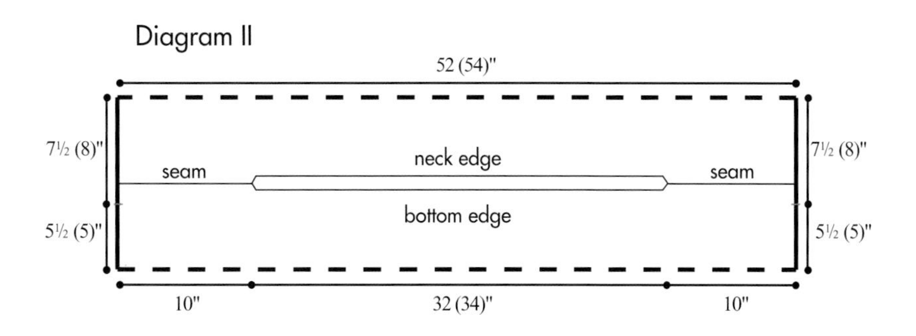

On the slopes, or by the fireplace sipping coffee, these toasty pieces will keep you warm and cuddly.

st.moritz

3 rectangles

st.moritz

SIZE

One size fits all.

MATERIALS

Dune by Trendsetter Yarns, 1¾oz/50g balls, each approx 90yd/83m (mohair/acrylic/viscose/nylon/metal)

- 3 balls in #30 Rust/Wine/Navy/Olive
- 1½yd/1.5m of 2¼"/5.5cm-wide light rust suede flower trim
- One pair each sizes 9 and 10 (5.5 and 6mm) needles or size to obtain gauge
- Matching sewing thread
- Sewing needle

GAUGE

16 sts to 4"/10cm over rib pat using smaller needles.

Take time to check gauge.

FINISHED MEASUREMENTS

Hat

Circumference 19"/48cm

3 rectangles

RIB PATTERN

Row 1 (RS) *K2, p2; rep from * to end.

Rep row 1 for rib pat.

REVERSE STOCKINETTE STITCH

Row 1 (RS) Purl.

Row 2 Knit.

Rep rows 1 and 2 for reverse St st.

HAT

Beg at bottom edge with smaller needles, cast on 76 sts. Work in rib pat for 3"/6.5cm, end with a WS row. Cont in reverse St st until piece measures 12"/30.5cm from beg. Bind off.

FINISHING

Sew back seam. Using Dune, sew a running stitch 3"/7.5cm down from top edge. Pull tight to gather; fasten off securely. Cut a 18"/45.5cm length of flower trim; 8 flowers. Sew on as shown or as desired.

GLOVES (make 2)

Beg at hand edge with smaller needles, cast on 32 sts. Work in rib pat for 2"/5cm. Mark beg and end of last row for beg of thumb opening. Work even for 2"/5cm. Mark beg and end of last row for end of thumb opening. Cont to work even until piece measures 15"/38cm from beg. Bind off in rib pat using larger needles.

FINISHING

For each glove, sew side seam leaving thumb opening unstitched. Cut a 15¼"/38.5cm length of flower trim; 6 flowers. Sew on as shown or as desired.

DESIGN OPTION

Add a strand of eyelash or lash yarn to hat for a fun look.

This shawl always looks great—by daylight or starlight.

stella

2 triangles

stella

MATERIALS

Sunshine by Trendsetter Yarns, 1¾oz/50g balls, each approx 95yd/87m (viscose/polyamide)

- 8 balls in #33 Periwinkle (A)

Aura by Trendsetter Yarns, 1¾oz/50g balls, each approx 148yd/135m (nylon)

- 4 balls in #3169 Grape (B)
- One pair size 7 (4.5mm) needles or size to obtain gauge
- Crochet hook size F/5 (3.75mm)
- Two 4 oz. bottles of Gel by Trendsetter Yarns (optional)
- One covered hook and eye set
- Matching sewing thread
- Sewing needle

GAUGE

18 sts to 4"/10cm over St st using size 7 (4.5mm) needles.

Take time to check gauge.

FINISHED MEASUREMENTS

Width across top edge 53"/134.5cm (not including fringe)

Length from back neck to bottom point 28"/71cm (not including fringe)

2 triangles

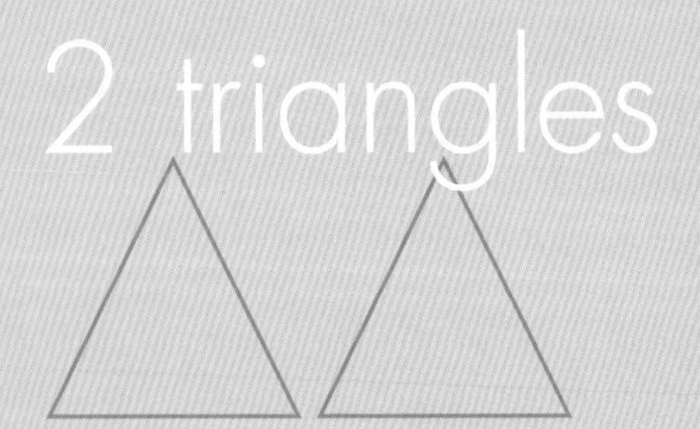

STOCKINETTE STITCH

Row 1 (RS) Knit.

Row 2 Purl.

Rep rows 1 and 2 for St st.

STRIPE PATTERN

Working in St st, *work 6 rows A and 4 rows B; rep from * (10 rows) for stripe pat.

TRIANGLES (make 2)

With A, cast on 119 sts. Cont in stripe pat and work dec row as foll:

Dec row (RS) K1, SKP, k across to last 3 sts, k2tog, k1—117 sts. Cont to work dec row every 4th row 57 times more. Bind off 3 rem sts.

FINISHING

Referring to diagram, place triangles side by side with cast-on edges at bottom. Sew back seam from A to B, leaving bottom 11"/28cm unstitched for neck opening.

Gelling

Gel contains bleach that will diffuse the dye in the yarn. Because it contains bleach, it is important to work on a surface that will not be affected by the gel. However, the surface should be flat and large enough to accommodate the size of the shawl.

Spread shawl out flat on work surface. Open up top of gel, then carefully squeeze out an even stream, in a swirl pattern, from outside edge toward center and opposite stripe pat. Repeat all over the shawl, using the second bottle when needed. Let gel remain on piece until desired diffusion is reached. Fill up a sink with cool water.

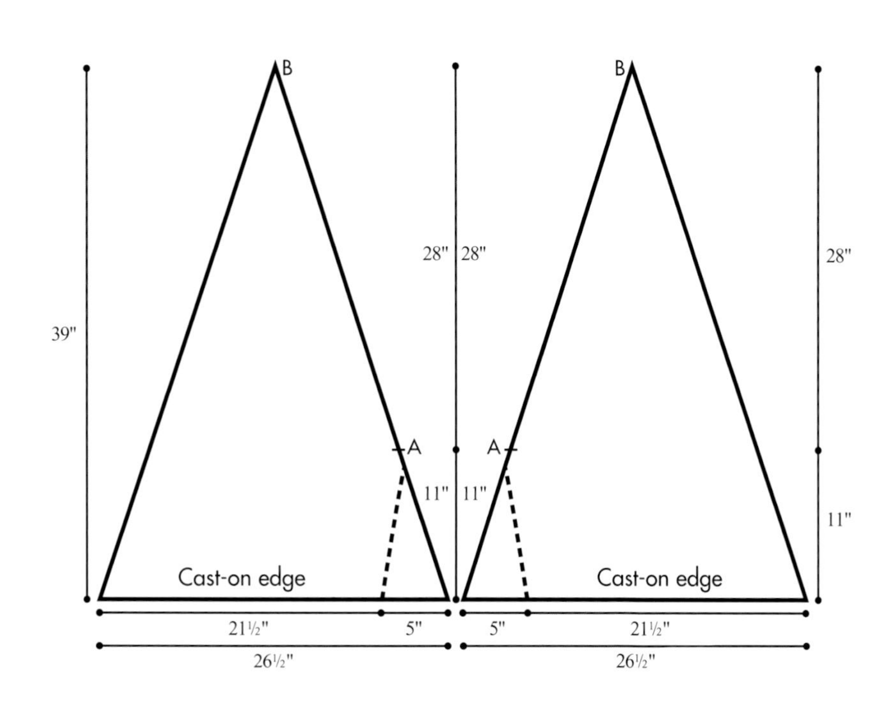

Rinse repeatedly until water runs clear. Squeeze out excess water; do not wring out. Cover a large flat surface with terry towels. Lay shawl flat on towels and let dry.

Edging

From RS and crochet hook, join A with a sl st in first row of side edge. **Row 1 (RS)** *Ch 3, sk next 2 rows of side edge, sl st in next row of side edge; rep from * to first row of opposite side edge. Fasten off.

Fringe

Cut rem A and B into 17"/43cm strands. For each fringe, fold 3 strands of A and 1 strand of B in half. With WS facing, use crochet hook to draw center of strands through first ch-3 sp of edging, forming a loop. Pull ends of fringe through this loop. Pull to tighten. Cont to make a fringe in every ch-3 sp along edging.

Collar

Referring to diagram, measure and mark 5"/12.5cm in from each neck edge. Fold each neck over to WS (following dash line) to within 1"/2.5cm of back seam. Using B, hem in place, then whipstitch side edges of collar tog. Fold collar over to RS along hem. Using sewing needle and thread, sew hook and eye set at base of collar.

DESIGN OPTIONS

- Attach fringe before gelling. Gelled fringe is really wonderful. Keep in mind you may need an extra bottle of gel.
- Gel works with all cottons, rayons or blends of cotton/rayon. Be sure to keep gel on long enough to see the diffusion.
- Fringe can be worked in any ribbon if you want a real open and light fringe.

It can be sweet, elegant or crazy. Whatever form it takes...shake your bon-bon.

bon-bon

2 rectangles

bon-bon

MATERIALS

Linea by Trendsetter Yarns, 1¾oz/50g balls, each approx 70yd/65m (polyester)

- 5 balls in #1468 Midnight (MC)

Segue by Trendsetter Yarns, 3½oz/100g hanks, each approx 120yd/110m (polyamide)

- 1 hank in #1337 Midnight Madness (CC)
- One pair size 11 (8mm) needles or size to obtain gauge
- Crochet hook size G/6 (4mm)
- 14"/35.5cm round pillow form
- Matching sewing thread
- Sewing needle

GAUGE

10 sts to 4"/10cm over reverse St st using MC size 11 (8mm) needles.

Take time to check gauge.

FINISHED MEASUREMENTS

14"/35.5cm diameter

2 rectangles

REVERSE STOCKINETTE STITCH

Row 1 (RS) Purl.

Row 2 Knit.

Rep rows 1 and 2 for reverse St st.

GARTER STITCH

Row 1 (RS) Knit.

Rep row 1 for garter st.

FRONT AND BACK

With MC, cast on 60 sts. Work in reverse St st until piece measures 40"/106.5 from beg. Bind off.

TIE

With CC, cast on 3 sts. Work in garter st until piece measures 24"/61 from beg. Bind off.

FINISHING

Sew short edges (cast on to bind off) of MC strip tog forming a ring.

Front rosette edging

From RS, join CC with a sl st in seam of MC ring. Rnd 1 *Ch 2, sl st in next st; rep from * around. Join rnd with a sl st in first sl st. Fasten off. Do not work for back rosette.

Rosettes

Cut a 40"/101.5cm strand of thread. Using thread doubled in sewing needle. Run a gathering thread 5"/12.5cm from front rosette edging. Pull tight to gather, then tightly wrap thread 3 times around base of gathers; fasten off securely. Insert pillow form. To close pillow cover, run a gathering thread 4"/10cm from edge of back rosette. Pull tight to gather, then tightly wrap thread 3 times around base of gathers; fasten off securely. Cut rem CC into 11"/28cm lengths. Tie on CC bows as shown or as desired. Tie the CC tie around base of front rosette.

DESIGN OPTIONS

- Make piece narrower so rosette is only on the front. Simply cast on 12 fewer stitches. Run a gathering thread through one edge and pull tight to gather in. Insert pillow form and create the Bon-Bon rosette with the remaining fabric on the front.
- Embellish like crazy with lots of beads and cut fabric.
- Make front rosette bigger by making first rosette smaller and pulling more towards the front.
- Work a strand of Trendsetter's Fireworks, a metallic eyelash yarn, along each edge to add sparkle to the rosettes.

Easy and glamorous, this matching set is the perfect outfit for home, travel and business.

lauren

4 rectangles

lauren

SIZES

Instructions for poncho are written for size Small. Changes for sizes Medium, Large and X-Large are in parentheses. Instructions for skirt are written for size Small/Medium. Changes for size Medium/Large is in parentheses.

MATERIALS

Charm by Trendsetter Yarns, .7oz/20g balls, each approx 94yd/86m (polyester/polyamide tactel)

Poncho

- 7 (9, 11, 13) balls in #80 Tapestry (A)

Skirt

- 7 (9) balls in #80 Tapestry (A)

Toreador by Lane Borgosesia/Trendsetter Yarns, .87oz/25g balls, each approx 198yd/180m (viscose/polyester)

Poncho

- 3 (4, 5, 6) balls in #157 Copper (B)

Skirt

- 3 (4) balls in #157 Copper (B)

Hannah Silk bias cut ribbon, ⅝"/16mm-wide, each spool approx 40yd/37m (silk)

- 1 spool in Tuscany (C)
- One pair size 9 (5.5mm) needles or size to obtain gauge
- Crochet hook size G/6 (4mm)
- 1yd/1m of 1"/2.5cm-wide elastic
- Matching sewing thread
- Sewing needle

GAUGE

20 sts to 4"/10cm over St st using A and B held tog and size 9 (5.5mm) needles.

Take time to check gauge.

FINISHED MEASUREMENTS

Poncho

Bust 47 (48, 49, 50)"/119.5 (122, 124.5, 127)cm

Length to bottom point 18 (19, 20, 21)"/45.5 (48, 51, 53.5)cm

Skirt

Hips 36 (42)"/91.5 (106.5)cm

Length 25½"/64.5cm

NOTES

1) Work with 1 strand each of A and B held tog throughout.

2) The vertical drop stitch pattern is created by unraveling stitches after knitting is completed.

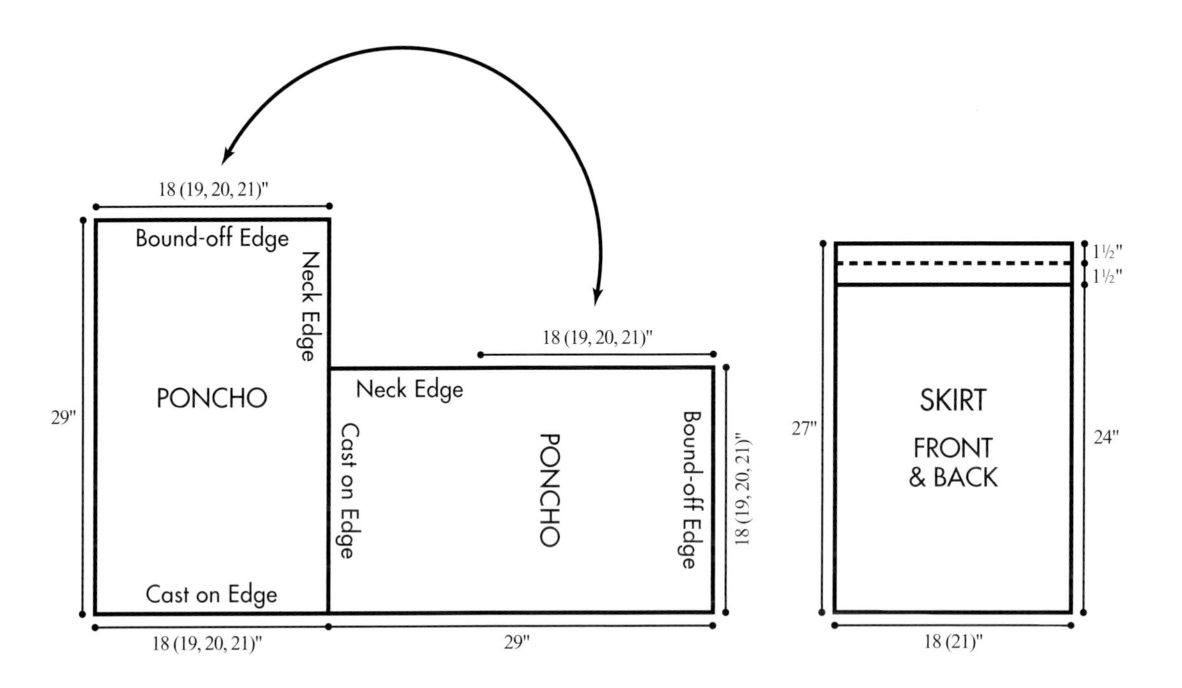

STOCKINETTE STITCH

Row 1 (RS) Knit.

Row 2 Purl.

Rep rows 1 and 2 for St st.

PONCHO (make 2)

With A and B held tog, cast on 77 (83, 89, 95) sts.

Foundation row (RS) *K4, k2tog, yo; rep from * end k5. Beg with a purl row, cont in St st until piece measures 29"/73.5cm, end with a WS row.

Last row (RS) *K5, drop next st off needle, yo; rep from *, end k5.

Bind off evenly.

Unraveling stitches

Carefully unravel each dropped stitch down to yo of foundation row. Pull piece in each direction to open up the horizontal strands.

FINISHING

From WS, carefully steam-block pieces following measurements; do not put steam iron directly onto knitting. Allow pieces to dry. Referring to diagram, sew cast-on edge of first piece to side edge of 2nd piece as shown. Sew bound-off edge of 2nd piece to side edge of first piece as shown. Butterfly-tie C (see page 11).

Neck edging

Position poncho so neck edge is at top and RS is facing you. Make a slip knot in end of C. Beg at a shoulder seam, insert crochet hook 1 st from top neck edge. On WS, place slip knot on hook and draw up to RS. Cont to work in slip st (see page 140) around entire neck edge, ending at beg shoulder seam. Fasten off. Push all butterfly ties to RS.

Outer edging

From RS, join C with a sl st in a shoulder seam. **Rnd 1** Ch 1, making sure that work lies flat, sc evenly around entire edge, working 2 sc in each corner. Join rnd with a sl st in first sc. Fasten off. Pull all butterfly ties to RS.

SKIRT (make 2)

With A and B held tog, cast on 83 (95) sts.

Foundation row (RS) *K4, k2tog, yo; rep from * end k5. Beg with a purl row, cont in St st until piece measures 24"/73.5cm, end with a WS row.

Next row (RS) *K5, drop next st off needle, yo; rep from *, end k5.

Waistband

Beg with a purl row, cont in St st for 1½"/4cm, end with a RS row. Knit next row for turning ridge. Cont in St st for 1½"/4cm more. Bind off loosely.

Unraveling stitches

Carefully unravel each dropped stitch down to yo of foundation row. Pull piece in each direction to open up the horizontal strands.

FINISHING

Steam-block pieces as for poncho; let dry. Sew side seams. Cut elastic 1"/2.5cm longer than desired waist measurement. For casing, turn waistband over to WS along turning ridge. Hem in place, leaving a 2"/5cm opening. Run elastic through casing, then overlap ends of elastic ½"/1.5cm; sew tog. Sew casing opening closed. Butterfly-tie C (see page 11).

Bottom edging

From RS, join C with a sl st in side seam. **Rnd 1** Ch 1, making sure that work lies flat, sc evenly around entire edge. Join rnd with a sl st in first sc. Fasten off. Pull all butterfly ties to RS.

DESIGN OPTIONS

- Make a simple shell using a solid color of Trendsetter's Sunshine, or another classic rayon yarn, to wear under this poncho to create a finished outfit.
- Run lengths of Hannah Silk ribbon through the horizontal strands of the unraveled stitches. Tie with bows at each end of work.
- Cut pieces of Hannah Silk ribbon, then tie into butterfly bows all over the poncho to embellish.
- Work skirt in one piece. Sew back seam leaving bottom 6"/15cm unstitched for a slit opening.

This sugary confection is a delight to knit and wear.

lollipop

5 rectangles

5 rectangles x five

lollipop

SIZES

Instructions are written for size Small. Changes for sizes Medium and Large are in parentheses.

MATERIALS

String of Pearls by Muench Yarns, 1¾oz/50g balls, each approx 99yd/91m (cotton/viscose/polyester)

- 2 balls each in #4014 Orange (A), #4004 Lime (D) and #4009 Turquoise (E)
- 5 (6, 6) balls in #4015 Plum (B)

Oceana by Muench Yarns, 1¾oz/50g balls, each approx 77yd/71m (viscose/nylon/cotton)

- 4 (5, 5) balls in #4802 Green (C)
- One pair each sizes 6, 7 and 8 (4, 4.5, 5mm) needles or size to obtain gauge
- Crochet hook size G/6 (4mm)

FINISHED MEASUREMENTS

Bust 46 (48, 50)"/117 (122, 127)cm

Length 20 (21, 21)"/51 (53.5, 53.5)cm

Upper arm 14 (14, 15)"/35.5 (35.5, 38)cm

GAUGE

16 sts and 24 rows to 4"/10cm over St st using size 8 (5mm) needles.

Take time to check gauge.

NOTES

1) Row gauge is extremely important so that stripe pat matches across shoulders.

2) Back and front are made horizontally from side to side.

3) Sleeves are made vertically from the bottom up.

4) When working outer edging, change colors by drawing the new color through 2 loops on hook to complete the last sc.

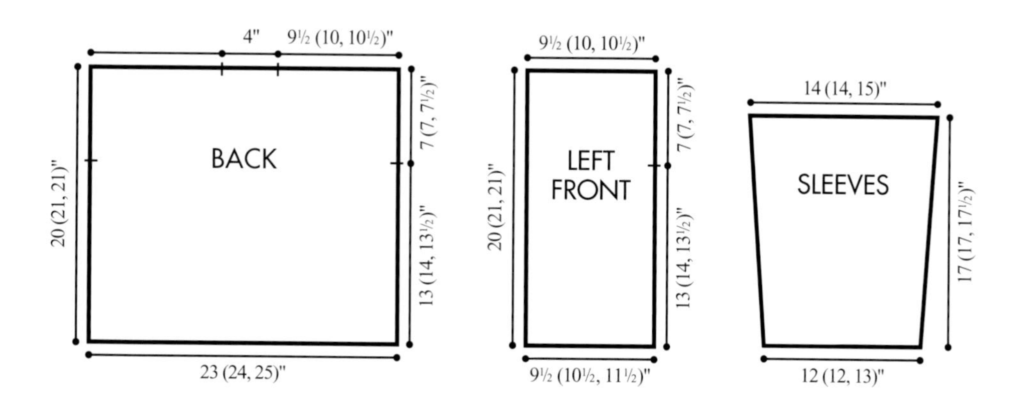

REVERSE STOCKINETTE STITCH

Row 1 (RS) Purl.

Row 2 Knit.

Rep rows 1 and 2 for reverse St st.

STRIPE PATTERN

Working in reverse St st, *2 rows A, 2 rows B, 2 rows C, 2 rows D, 2 rows E and 2 rows C; rep from * (12 rows) for stripe pat.

BACK

Beg at left side edge, with size 8 needles and A, cast on 80 (84, 84) sts. Cont in reverse St st and stripe pat for 138 (144, 152) rows. Piece should measure 19 (21, 23)"/58.5 (61, 63.5)cm from beg. Bind off for left side edge.

LEFT FRONT

Beg at side edge, with size 8 needles and A, cast on 80 (84, 84) sts. Cont in reverse St st and stripe pat for 56 (60, 64) rows. Piece measure approx 9½ (10½, 11½)"/24 (25.5, 26.5)cm from beg. Bind off for front edge. Make note of next color in stripe pat.

RIGHT FRONT

Beg at front edge, with size 8 needles and using next color in stripe pat, cast on 80 (84, 84) sts. Cont to work as for left front.

SLEEVES

With size 6 needles and B, cast on 56 (56, 60) sts. Work in reverse St st for 6 rows. Cont in reverse St st and work in stripe pat as foll: 2 rows E, 2 rows D, 2 rows C and 2 rows A. Change to B and work even until piece measures 5"/12.5cm from beg. Change to size 7 needles and work even until piece measures 10"/25.5cm from beg. Change to size 8 needles and work even until piece measures 17 (17, 17½)"/43 (43, 44.5)cm from beg, end with a WS row. Bind off.

FINISHING

Sew shoulder seams matching stripes. Place markers 7 (7, 7½)"/17.5 (17.5, 19)cm down from shoulders. Sew sleeves to armholes between markers. Sew side and sleeve seams.

Outer edging

From RS, with crochet hook, join same color as last stripe of left front with a sl st in center back neck.

Rnd 1 Ch 1, making sure that work lies flat, sc evenly around to center back bottom edge. Join same color as first stripe of right front. Cont to sc around to center back neck edge.

Rnd 2 Ch 1, working from left to right, reverse sc in each st around to center back bottom edge. Change to other color, then cont to work in reverse sc to center back neck. Join rnd with a sl st in first st. Fasten off both colors.

Front trim

Trim is worked in chain st, between sc of rnds 1 and 2 of edging. Take care to maintain st and row gauge as you work. Position jacket so back neck edge is at top and RS is facing you. Make a slip knot in end of color used for left front. Insert hook between first 2 sc of that color. On WS, place slip knot on hook and draw up to RS. Insert hook between next 2 sc and draw up a loop, then draw through loop on hook–first chain st made. Insert hook between next 2 sc and draw up a loop, then draw through loop on hook–2nd chain st made. Working from right to left, cont to work chain st, changing to next color when you reach center back bottom edge. Cont until you reach center back neck edge, then fasten off.

Sleeve edging

From RS, with crochet hook, join B with a sl st in underarm seam.

Rnd 1 Ch 1, working from left to right, sc in each st around. Join rnd with a sl st in first st. Fasten off.

DESIGN OPTIONS

- Work stripes throughout the complete jacket and start at one cuff and work across from sleeve to sleeve.
- Make a sleeveless shell to go underneath the jacket to complete the suit.

Thick and thin yarn, together with paillettes, make you the shining star.

luminary

1 rectangle

1 rectangle

luminary

MATERIALS

Segue by Trendsetter Yarns, 3½oz/100g hanks, each approx 120yd/110m (polyamide)

- 1 hank in #1337 Midnight Madness (A)

Joy by Trendsetter Yarns, .87oz/25g balls, each approx 65yd/60m (polyamide/polyester)

- 2 balls in #1337 Midnight Madness (B)

Ruffles large paillettes by Trendsetter Yarns, each 10 pieces per box

- 1 box each in #M19 Copper, #M69 Brown, #M72 Plum and #MI44 Purple
- One pair size 13 (9mm) needles or size to obtain gauge
- Crochet hook size F/5 (3.75mm)

GAUGE

Gauge is not important to the success of this scarf as it is made by alternating a thick ribbon yarn and a thin component yarn.

FINISHED MEASUREMENTS

Approximately 5" x 60"/13.5 x 154.5cm (not including fringe)

NOTE

When working stripe pat, carry color not in use loosely along side edge of work.

GARTER STITCH

Row 1 (RS) Knit.

Rep row 1 for garter st.

STRIPE PATTERN

Working in garter st, *work 2 rows B and 2 rows A; rep from * (4 rows) for stripe pat.

PAILETTE STITCH

Always worked on first row of A stripe. Insert crochet hook into pailette hole. From RS, insert the hook into the next st on left-hand needle as if to knit. Yo hook and draw yarn through the stitch and pailette. Slip this st off left-hand needle onto hook, then transfer this st from hook onto right-hand needle.

SCARF

With A, cast on 15 sts. Knit next row.

Change to B and knit next 2 rows.

Change to A.

Placing and spacing paillettes

Next row (RS) K2, using pailette colors as desired, work pailette st in next st, k5, work pailette st in next st, k6.

Next row Knit. Change to B and cont in stripe pat, adding paillettes until they are all used up as foll: alternate working pailette st on every A stripe, every other A stripe or every 3rd A stripe as desired, spreading colors around as desired. On first row of A stripes, place 1 or 2 paillettes randomly spaced across the row to add to the overall random design. For best results, work pailette st at least 2 sts from side edges. When B has run out, end with one row of A. Bind off knitwise.

Fringe

Cut rem A into 15"/38cm strands. Fold one strand in half. With WS facing, use hook to draw center of strand through first st of cast-on edge, forming a loop. Pull ends of fringe through this loop. Pull to tighten. Cont to make a fringe in every st along cast-on edge. Fringe bound-off edge in the same manner.

Shapely, sexy and youthful.

dusty

4 rectangles

dusty

SIZES

Instructions are written for size Petite. Changes for sizes Small, Medium and Large are in parentheses.

MATERIALS

Montage by Trendsetter Yarns, 1¾oz/50g balls, each approx 110yd/101m (polyamide/viscose/polyester)

- 6 (7, 8, 9) balls in #1231 Orange/Pink/Gold (MC)

Hannah Silk bias cut ribbon, 1"/25mm-wide, each spool approx 40yd/37m (silk)

- 1 spool in Echinacea (CC)
- One pair each sizes 6, 7 and 8 (4, 4.5, 5mm) needles or size to obtain gauge
- Crochet hook size F/5 (3.75mm)

GAUGE

17 sts and 21 rows to 4"/10cm over St st using MC and size 8 (5mm) needles.

Take time to check gauge.

FINISHED MEASUREMENTS

Bust 32 (36, 40, 44)"/81 (91.5, 101.5, 111.5)cm

Length 18 (19, 20, 20)"/45.5 (48, 51, 51)cm

Upper arm 14 (15, 16, 17)"/35.5 (38, 40.5, 43)cm

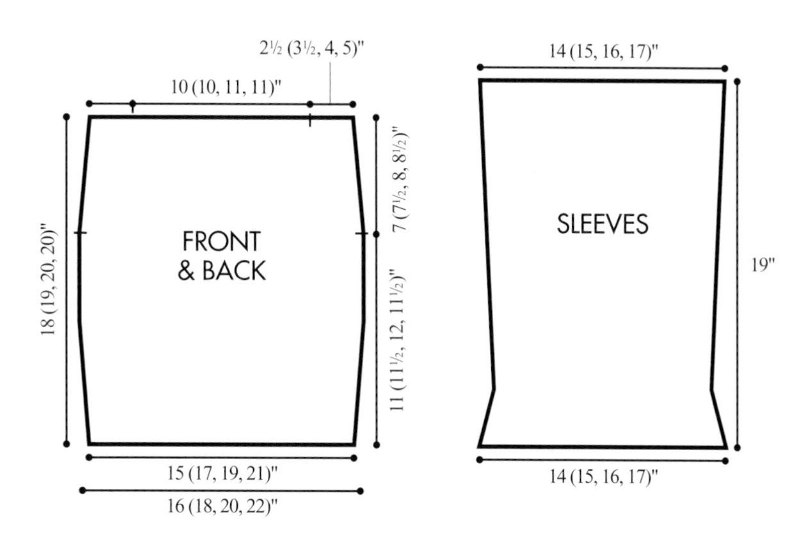

STOCKINETTE STITCH

Row 1 (RS) Knit.

Row 2 Purl.

Rep rows 1 and 2 for St st.

BACK

With size 6 needles and MC, cast on 68 (76, 86, 94) sts. Cont in St st for 3"/7.5cm. Change to size 7 needles and work even until piece measures 7"/17.5cm from beg. Change to size 8 needles and work even until piece measures 11"/28cm from beg. Mark each end. Change to size 7 needles and work even until piece measures 14"/35.5cm from beg. Change to size 6 needles and work even until piece measures 18 (19, 20, 20)"/45.5 (48, 51, 51)cm from beg, end with a WS row. Bind off.

FRONT

Work as for back.

SLEEVES

With size 8 needles and MC, cast on 60 (64, 68, 72) sts. Cont in St st for 3"/7.5cm, end with a WS row.

Eyelet row (RS) K1 (3, 1, 3), *yo, k2tog, k5; rep from *, end yo, k2tog, k1 (3, 1, 3).

Next row Purl. Change to size 6 needles and cont in St st until piece measures 8"/20.5cm from beg. Change to size 7 needles and work even until piece measures 13"/33cm from beg. Change to size 8 needles and work even until piece measures 19"/51cm from beg, end with a WS row. Bind off.

FINISHING

Sew a 2½ (3½, 4, 5)"/6.5 (9, 10, 12.5)cm shoulder seam each side, leaving center 10 (10, 11, 11)"/25.5 (25.5, 28, 28)cm open at center for neck opening. Sew sleeves to armholes between markers. Sew side and sleeve seams.

Prepare ribbon

Cut out all seams from CC (see page 11). At this point, butterfly-tie only enough ribbon for neck edging.

Neck edging

Position sweater so neck edge is at top and RS is facing you. Make a slip knot in end of butterfly-tied CC. Beg at a shoulder seam, insert hook 1 st from top neck edge. On WS, place slip knot on hook and draw up to RS. Cont to work in slip st (see page 140) around entire neck edge, ending at beg shoulder seam. Fasten off. Pull all butterfly ties to RS.

Loop stitch collar

You will using separate strips of CC without joining them. Working from the WS, join CC with a sl st in center back slip stitch. **Rnd 1** *Insert hook into next st. Place CC over left index finger, then position finger about 2"/2.5cm away edging. Use hook to catch free end of CC and draw through st. Drop loop from finger. Taking care not to change length of loop, yo and draw through 2 loops on hook to complete a sc. Pull tightly on loop to secure; rep from * around using a new strip of CC whenever necessary. Join rnd with a sl st in first st. Fasten off. Cut two 22"/56cm long strips of CC and set aside for wrist ties. Butterfly-tie rem CC for bottom and sleeve edgings.

Bottom edging

From RS, join CC with a sl st in left side seam.

Rnd 1 Sl st in each st around. Join rnd with a sl st in first sl st. Fasten off. Pull all butterfly ties to RS.

Sleeve edging

From RS, join CC with a sl st in underarm seam. Cont to work as for bottom edging. Weave ribbon through eyelets, beg and ending at center of sleeve. Gather sleeve, then tie ribbon in a bow. Pull all butterfly ties to RS.

DESIGN OPTIONS

■ Make a narrow matching scarf or belt. With size 10 (6mm) needles and Montage, cast on 7 sts. Work in garter stitch (knit every row) until the piece measures about 50"/127cm long. Bind off. Cut Hannah Silk into 5"/12.5cm lengths, then tie into butterfly bows (see page 11) in a carefree design on the right side.

■ To create a more boxy silhouette for a fuller figure, work the front and back using the size 8 (5mm) needles only. If necessary, make the body longer and leave the bottom 3"/7.5cm on each side seam open to allow added ease for the hips. Be sure to make the sleeves slightly shorter as dropped shoulders add length to sleeves.

■ This design would make a wonderful shell to wear under a suit. Simply follow the instructions for the front and back only. Trim the armholes with single crochet using the Hannah Silk ribbon and enjoy.

Fun, fantastical or formal, this triangle-shaped pillow sets any mood.

trillow

trillow

MATERIALS

Merino Otto by Lane Borgosesia/Trendsetter Yarns, 1¾oz/50g balls, each approx 130yd/125m (wool)

- 4 balls in #26929 Blue (A) for pillow, 1 extra ball for optional tassels

Swing by Trendsetter Yarns, 1¾oz/50g balls, each approx 65yd/60m (polyamide/tactel nylon/lurex)

- 2 balls in #1841 Blue/Green (B) for pillow, 1 extra ball for optional tassels
- One pair size 8 (5mm) needles or size to obtain gauge
- 6"/15cm square (for optional tassels) and 12"/30.5cm square (for pillow) of heavyweight cardboard
- One large bag of polyester fiberfill

GAUGE

20 sts and 26 rows to 4"/10cm over St st using A and size 8 (5mm) needles.

Take time to check gauge.

FINISHED MEASUREMENTS

12" x 12" x 8"/30.5 x 30.5 x 20/5cm

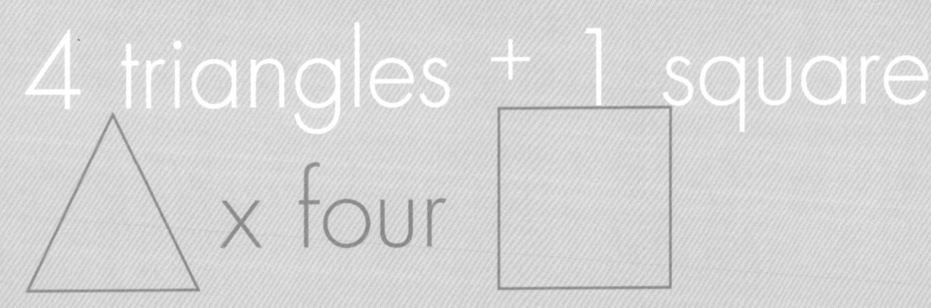

STOCKINETTE STITCH

Row 1 (RS) Knit.

Row 2 Purl.

Rep rows 1 and 2 for St st.

GARTER STITCH

Row 1 (RS) Knit.

Rep row 1 for garter st.

STRIPE PATTERN I

*With A, work in St st for 12 rows, with B work in garter st for 12 rows; rep from * (24 rows) for stripe pat I.

STRIPE PATTERN II

*With B, work in garter st for 12 rows, with A work in St st for 12 rows; rep from * (24 rows) for stripe pat II.

FRONT

Triangles 1 and 3

With A, cast on 58 sts. Work in stripe pat I, AT SAME TIME, dec as foll:

Dec row (RS) K1, SKP, k across to last 3 sts, k2tog, k1—56 sts. Cont to work dec row every other row 26 times more. Bind off 4 rem sts.

Triangles 2 and 4

With B, cast on 58 sts. Work in stripe pat II, AT SAME TIME, cont to work as for triangles 1 and 3.

BASE

With A, cast on 58 sts. Work in garter st until piece measures 12"/30.5cm from beg. Bind off.

FINISHING

Sew cast on edge of triangle 1 to cast on edge of base. Sew cast on edge of triangle 3 to bind off edge of base. Sew cast on edges of triangles 2 and 4 to open edges of base. Sew side edges of triangles together leaving the top open. Insert 12" square cardboard into base. Cover with fiberfill until firm. Sew balance of top closed.

Tassels (make 4)

With A and B held tog, wrap 25 times around 6"/15cm square of cardboard. Slip an 8"/20.5cm-length of A under strands and tightly knot at one end of cardboard. Remove cardboard. Wrap and tie another length of A around the tassel about 1½"/4cm down from the top. Cut loops at opposite ends. Trim ends even. Sew a tassel to each corner; as shown.

DESIGN OPTIONS

- To make the pillow bigger or smaller, simply start with more or less stitches for the base. Triangles have the same number of stitches as the base and the decreases will continue to be every other row. Note that with more stitches, the height of the triangle will increase. With fewer stitches, the height of the triangle will decrease.
- Embellish the triangle, if desired, by making some wonderful tassels to adorn each corner of the base. The top of the triangle can be left open allowing each point to fold over. A smaller tassel can hang off each point. Just have fun.

This coverup is so quick and easy...which color will you make next?

goldie

SIZES

One size fits all. Instructions are written for Small sleeve width and length. Changes for Medium and Large sleeve widths and lengths are in parentheses.

MATERIALS

Blossom by Trendsetter Yarns, 1¾oz/50g balls, each approx 92yd/84m (polyamide/viscose)

- 4 (5, 6) balls in #106 Olive (MC)

Joy by Trendsetter Yarns, .87oz/25g balls, each approx 65yd/60m (polyamide/polyester)

- 5 balls in #123 Sage (CC)
- Size 9 (5.5mm) circular needle, 36"/91.5cm long or size to obtain gauge
- One pair size 9 (5.5mm) needles or size to obtain gauge

GAUGE

14 sts to 4"/10cm over reverse St st using MC and size 9 (5.5mm) circular needle.

Take time to check gauge.

FINISHED MEASUREMENTS

Bust 52"/132cm

Length 14 (16, 18)"/35.5 (40.5, 45.5)cm

Upper arm 14 (16, 18)"/35.5 (40.5, 45.5)cm

NOTES

1) Work with 2 strands of CC held tog throughout.

2) Shrug body is worked in one piece.

4 rectangles x four

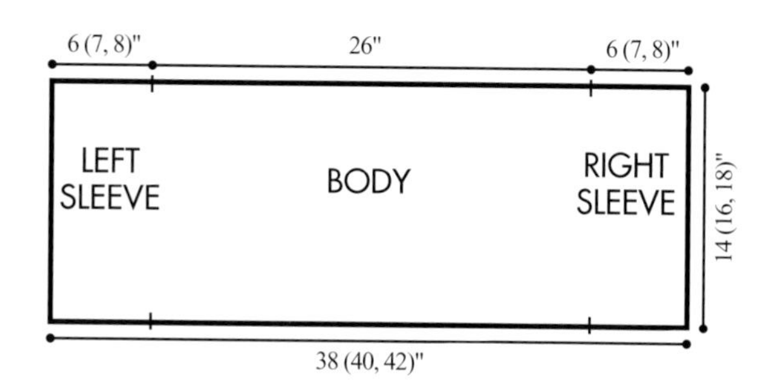

STOCKINETTE STITCH

Row 1 (RS) Knit.

Row 2 Purl.

Rep rows 1 and 2 for St st.

REVERSE STOCKINETTE STITCH

Row 1 (RS) Purl.

Row 2 Knit.

Rep rows 1 and 2 for reverse St st.

SLEEVES AND BODY

With circular needle and MC, cast on 50 (56, 64) sts. Do not join. Work back and forth in rev St st until piece measures 38 (40,42)" from beg. Bind off.

COLLAR

With straight needles and 2 strands of CC held tog, cast on 16 sts. Work even in reverse St st until piece measures 26"/66cm from beg. Bind off.

CUFFS (make 2)

With straight needles and 2 strands of CC held tog, cast on 9 sts. Work even in reverse St st until piece measures 14 (16, 18)"/35.5 (40.5, 45.5)cm from beg. Bind off.

FINISHING

Across each long edge of sleeves/body piece, measure and mark 6 (7, 8)"/15 (17.5, 20.5)cm in from each side edge. Fold in half lengthwise and sew side edges from edge to marker. Sew on collar to upper body edge between markers taking care that RS of collar is facing out when collar is folded over. Sew cuff to sleeve edge.

DESIGN OPTIONS

- Stripe the body all the way through, changing stitch patterns from Stockinette stitch to garter stitch (knit every row) to create an interesting design.
- Work the design all in one yarn.
- Reverse yarns to have a fun, furry body and classic collar and cuffs.

Whether it's in the North or South, this Dakota scarf always looks great.

dakota

1 rectangle

1 rectangle

dakota

MATERIALS

Checkmate by Trendsetter Yarns, 1¾oz/50g balls, each approx 70yd/64m (nylon)

- 3 balls in #1038 Peacock (A)

Vintage by Trendsetter Yarns, 1¾oz/50g balls, each approx 95yd/87m (polyester/tactel nylon)

- 2 balls in #1038 Peacock (B)
- One pair size 13 (9mm) needles or size to obtain gauge
- Crochet hook size G/6 (4mm)

GAUGE

12 sts to 4"/10cm over St st using size 13 (9mm) needles.

Take time to check gauge.

FINISHED MEASUREMENTS

6" x 78"/15 x 198cm

STOCKINETTE STITCH

Row 1 (RS) Knit.

Row 2 Purl.

Rep rows 1 and 2 for St st.

REVERSE STOCKINETTE STITCH

Row 1 (RS) Purl.

Row 2 Knit.

Rep rows 1 and 2 for reverse St st.

SCARF

With A, cast on 18 sts. Knit next row. Work first half of scarf as foll: *Change to B and work in St st for 3"/7.5cm, change to A and work in St st for 3". End with a RS row. Knit next WS row*. Repeat * to *3x total. *change to B and St st for 3" end with a RS row. Change to A, knit first WS row. Continue in stock st by knitting next (RS) row until 3". *Repeat * x * 3x total. Change to B and St st for 3", end with RS row. Change to A and knit next WS row. Bind off.

Fringe

Cut A into 13"/33cm strands. With RS of cast-on edge at your right, insert hook, from right to left, under first loop of first st of garter st ridge. Fold one strand in half. Draw center of strand through, forming a loop. Pull ends of strands through this loop, then pull to tighten. Cont to make a fringe in every st of garter st ridge. Working towards your left, knot fringe in next two garter st ridges. Turn scarf so that bound-off edge is at your right. Working as before, knot fringe in three rem garter st ridges.

Cashmere and silk come together in a soft rib with fur trim.

olivia

1 rectangle

2 rectangles

olivia

SIZE

One size fits all.

MATERIALS

Kashmir by Trendsetter Yarns, 1¾oz/50g balls, each approx 110yd/101m (cashmere/silk)

- 7 balls in #79 Olive (MC)

Bunny by Trendsetter Yarns, each ball approx 10yd/9.5m (rabbit)

- 1 ball in Khaki (CC)
- One pair size 10 (6mm) needles or size to obtain gauge
- Crochet hook size H/8 (5mm)

GAUGE

16 sts to 4"/10cm over rib pat (slightly stretched) using MC and size 10 (6mm) needles.

Take time to check gauge.

FINISHED MEASUREMENTS

Bust (closed) 48"/122cm

Length 19"/48cm

RIB PATTERN I

Row 1 (RS) *K6, p6; rep from *, end k6.

Row 2 *P6, k6; rep from *, end p6.

Rep rows 1 and 2 for rib pat I.

RIB PATTERN II

Row 1 (RS) P3, *k6, p6; rep from *, end k6, p3.

Row 2 K3, *p6, k6; rep from *, end p6, k3.

Rep rows 1 and 2 for rib pat II.

FRONTS AND UPPER BACK

With MC, cast on 66 sts. Work in rib pat I until piece measures 54"/137cm from beg. Bind off in rib pat.

LOWER BACK PANEL

With MC, cast on 72 sts. Work in rib pat II until piece measures 11"/28cm from beg. Bind off in rib pat.

FINISHING

Referring to diagram I, center bound-off edge of lower back panel along edge of fronts/upper back piece; sew in place. Referring to diagram II, bring side edge of left front to side edge of lower back panel, matching As and Bs. Sew 8"/20.5cm side seam (from A to B), leaving rem 10"/25.5cm edge of left front and rem 3"/7.5cm edge of lower back panel unstitched for armhole. Rep for right front.

Front trim

Trim is worked in chain st, 1 st from edge all around. Take care to maintain st and row gauge as you work. Position vest so front edge of right front is at top and RS is facing you. Make a slip knot in end of CC. Insert hook 1 st from front edge and between rows 1 and 2 from bottom edge. On WS, place slip knot on hook and draw up to RS. Insert hook between rows 5 and 6 and draw up a loop, then draw through loop on hook—first chain st made. Insert hook between rows 9 and 10 and draw up a loop, then draw through loop on hook—2nd chain st made. Working from right to left, cont to work a chain st over every 4 rows to bottom edge of left front. Fasten off.

Armhole trim

Work as for front trim, beg and ending at side seam.

Bottom trim

Position vest so bottom edge is at top and RS is facing you. Make a slip knot in end of MC. Insert hook 1 row from top edge and between first and 2nd sts from RH edge. On WS, place slip knot on hook and draw up to RS. Insert hook between 2nd and 3rd sts and draw up a loop, then draw through loop on hook–first chain st made. Insert hook between 3rd and 4th sts and draw up a loop, then draw through loop on hook—2nd chain st made.

olivia

Working from right to left, cont in chain st to LH edge. Fasten off.

DESIGN OPTIONS

- Work in stripes of different widths as they will look beautiful when wrapped around the body.
- Instead of Bunny, use a long lash yarn to work chain stitch around all the edges.

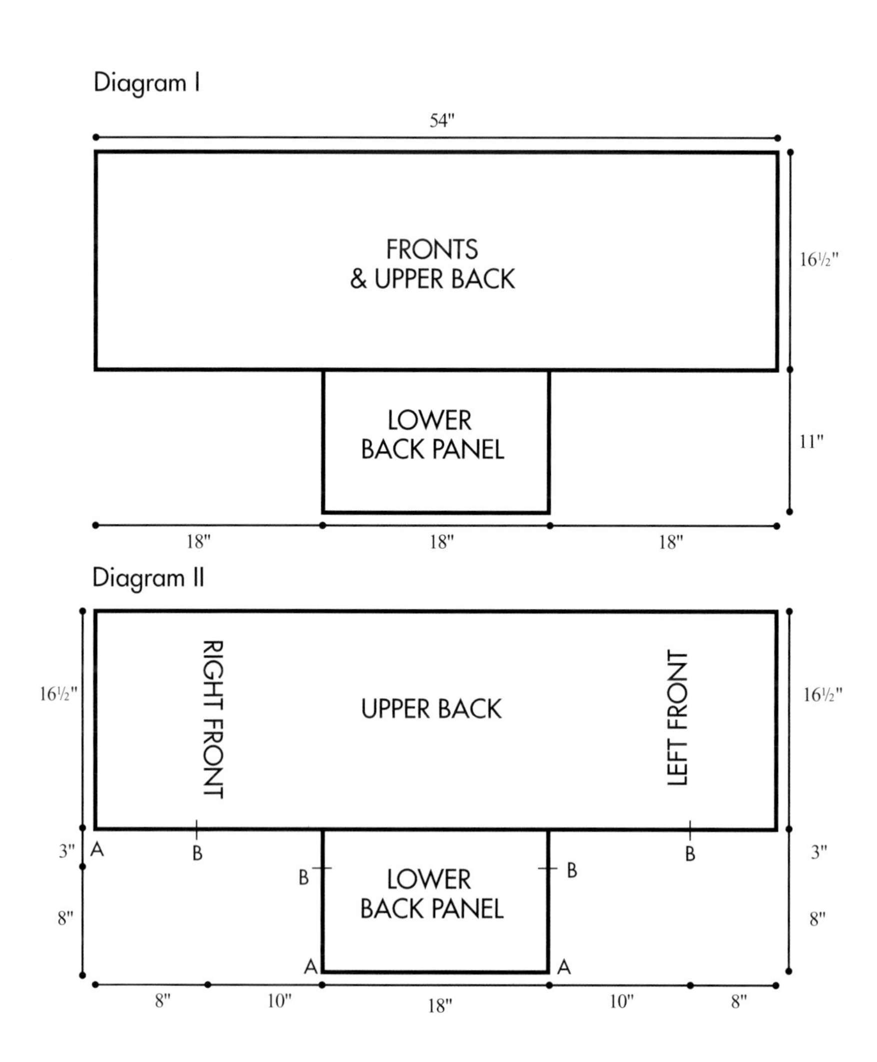

Fill it with more yarn to make another purse. Make two handles or just one.

purcy

MATERIALS

Liberty by Trendsetter Yarns, 1¾oz/50g balls, each approx 65yd/60m (wool/polyamide/acrylic)

- 3 balls in #961 Purple/Pink/Yellow (A)

Aura Print Trendsetter Yarns, 1¾oz/50g balls, each approx 145yd/133m (nylon)

- 2 balls in #1 Jelly Bean (B)

Merino Otto by Lane Borgosesia/Trendsetter Yarns, 1¾oz/50g balls, each approx 130yd/125m (wool)

- 2 balls in #26902 Lavender (C)
- One pair size 15 (10mm) needles or size to obtain gauge

GAUGE

10 sts to 4"/10cm over St st using A, B and C held tog and size 15 (10mm) needles.

Take time to check gauge.

FINISHED MEASUREMENTS

12" x 11"/30.5 x 28cm (not including handles)

NOTES

1) Work with 1 strand each of A, B and C held tog throughout.

2) Bag is made in one piece, beg and ending at bottom edge of bag.

1 rectangle

STOCKINETTE STITCH

Row 1 (RS) Knit.

Row 2 Purl.

Rep rows 1 and 2 for St st.

BAG

With 1 strand each of A, B and C held tog, cast on 30sts. Work in St st until piece measures 11"/28cm from beg.

Divide for handles

Next row (RS) K15, join another strand each of A, B and C, work to end. Working both sides at once, work even until piece measures 28"/71cm from beg.

Joining

Next row (RS) K across, dropping 2nd group of yarns. Cont to work even until piece measures 39"/99cm from beg. Bind off.

FINISHING

Sew bottom seam. Sew a 11"/28cm side seam each side. Embellish the bag as desired with a silk flower, beads, etc. Carry as shown, or if you want to close the bag, insert the RH handle through the LH handle, then slide the LH handle down so it lays horizontally. Carry the bag with the RH handle.

DESIGN OPTIONS

■ To make a larger or smaller bag, cast on more or less stitches depending on the desired size. Work first side of bag to desired length. Divide for handles and work until handles are about 1"/2.5cm to 1½"/4cm shorter than the length of the bag. Work second side of bag to match the first.

■ If you wish to make a shoulder bag that can be worn slung across the body, work one handle until it is 17"/43cm, end with a WS row; place these stitches on a holder. Continue with the other handle until it is 40"/101.5cm, end with a WS row. Place stitches from holder back on left-hand needle. Knit next row, dropping 2nd group of yarns. Work for 10½"/26.5cm more; bind off. Sew seams. To close the bag, insert the longer handle through the shorter handle. Carry the bag by slipping the longer handle over your head and one arm.

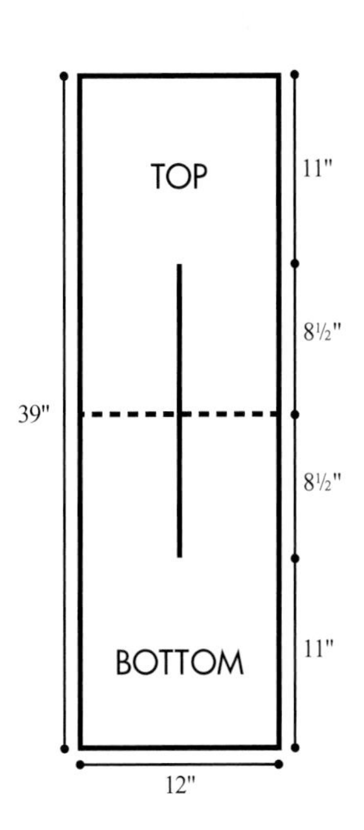

Textures and colors conspire to keep you all wrapped up.

wrapped up

1 rectangle

wrapped up

MATERIALS

Dune by Trendsetter Yarns, 1¾oz/50g balls, each approx 95yd/87m (mohair/acrylic/viscose/nylon/metal)

- 2 balls in #45 Brown/Olive/Yellow (A)

Checkmate by Trendsetter Yarns, 1¾oz/50g balls, each approx 70yd/64m (polyamide/tactel nylon)

- 3 balls in #811 Brown/Olive/Yellow (B)

Joy by Trendsetter Yarns, .87oz/25g balls, each approx 65yd/60m (polyamide/polyester)

- 3 balls in #1332 Mossy Tree (C)

Aura Print by Trendsetter Yarns, 1¾oz/50g balls, each approx 148yd/135m (nylon)

- 1 ball in #8294 Capuccino (D)

Bugia by Trendsetter Yarns, 1¾oz/50g balls, each approx 85yd/78m (nylon)

- 2 balls in #811 Brown/Beige/Olive (E)

Montage by Trendsetter Yarns, 1¾oz/50g balls, each approx 110yd/101m (polyamide/viscose/polyester)

- 2 balls in #1230 Brown/Olive/Copper (F)
- One pair size 11 (8mm) needles
- Crochet hook size G/6 (4mm)

GAUGE

Gauge is not important as each yarn is worked for only 1 row at a time. The differences in yarn thicknesses and textures create the unique look of this wrap.

FINISHED MEASUREMENTS

Approximately 20" x 50" to 55"/51 x 127 to 139.5cm (not including fringe)

1 rectangle

DASH RIB

Row 1 (RS) Knit.

Row 2 *K10, p10; rep from *, end k10.

Rep rows 1 and 2 for dash rib.

CUT AND TIE SIDE FRINGE

Work every row as foll: At end of row, cut yarn leaving a 4"/10cm tail. Leave 4" tail for next color and work the row. Secure tails every row with an overhand knot* at top.

WRAP

With A, cast on 70 sts. Cut yarn leaving a 4"/10cm tail, then tie on B foll cut and tie side fringe. Cont in dash rib and work in stripe pat as foll: Work 1 row each using C, D, E, F, A and B. Work even until piece measures 50" to 55"/127 to 139.5cm from beg. Bind off in dash rib.

Fringe

Cut rem B into 17"/43cm strands. Fold one strand in half. With WS facing, use crochet hook to draw center of strand through first st of cast-on edge, forming a loop. Pull ends of fringe through this loop. Pull to tighten. Cont to make a fringe in every st along cast-on edge. Fringe bound-off edge in the same manner. Trim all fringe evenly, or allow different lengths to play a part in the of the textural detail.

DESIGN OPTIONS

■ To make as a scarf, cast on half the number of stitches and work on size 10 (6mm) needles to give the knitted fabric more body.

■ Keep this idea in mind to create a wonderful jacket or pullover. Working with many different yarns, each for one row, allow textures and colors to play equal roles in the design. It's also a great way to use up lots of odd skeins of leftover yarn. Remember that big differences in gauge are again not important because each yarn is worked for only for one row.

PIECING IT TOGETHER

You are almost there! The pieces have been knitted and they look great. Now you need to put them together. For many of you scarf knitters, the only form of finishing you've had to do was bury some yarn tails. For the designs in this book, the pieces need to come together to form the finished project. Let's hope you kept your swatch and remember how the yarn reacts to steam and light stretching. If you don't no need to panic; just work one step at a time.

Blocking

We recommend that you block all of your pieces once they are knitted. This gives you the opportunity to uncurl the edges and to straighten out any piece that may need it. You should use a clean, flat surface. Some of you may have a blocking board or a blocking table which is even better. Read the yarn label to see what the manufacturer recommends. No matter what you do, just be careful.

Place one of the knitted pieces flat on the blocking surface with the wrong side facing up. Using a tape measure, pin it to the width and length as stated or shown on the schematics. Run a lukewarm steam iron over it, but do not press down or apply too much heat. You should be able to see a light mist on the yarn. Allow the piece to dry thoroughly; remove the pins. Continue to block pieces until all are done. Now you are ready to put them together!

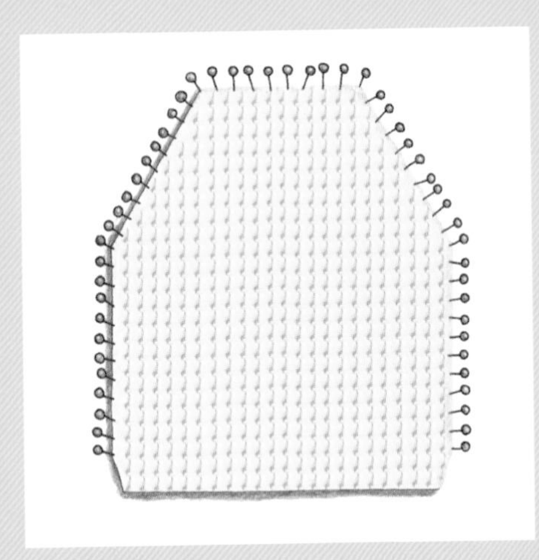

Sewing Seams

There are a couple of different ways to join seams together. Everyone you ask will tell you their own favorite way. Here are our two favorites. They are easy to do and will give your garment joinings that are seamless and durable.

The horizontal seam on Stockinette stitch method is the most seamless way to join shoulders, or any two bound-off edges, together. For best results you must have the same number of stitches on each piece so that the finished seam will resemble a continuous row or knit stitches. Simply butt the bound-off edges, lining up stitches from one side with stitches on opposite side. Insert the yarn needle under a stitch inside the bound-off edge of one side and then under the corresponding stitch on the other side. Repeat all the way across the join, making sure to pull the yarn tight enough to hide the bound-off edges.

Horizontal seam on St st

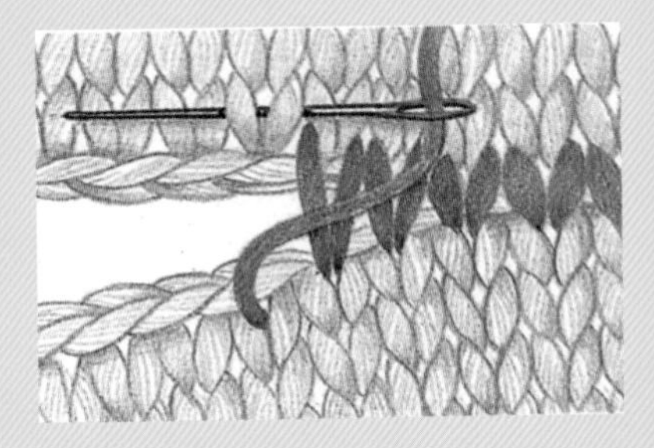

For vertical seams, as well as all other seams, we recommend the mattress stitch (also called weaving stitch). To sew, place the two pieces side by side (so stitches run in the same direction), the right sides are facing and bottom edges even. Begin at the bottom edge using the tail left over from casting on. If you don't have a tail long enough for sewing, attach a length of yarn securely to the selvedge. Insert the yarn needle under 2 horizontal bars between the first and second stitches from the edge, then under 2 stitches at the same place on the opposite piece. Pull the yarn up and away from you to close the seam. Continue working back and forth from side to side, moving up 2 horizontal bars at a time for about 6 moves on each side. Holding onto both pieces at the bottom, carefully pull the yarn up and away from you to close the seam.

Vertical seam on St st

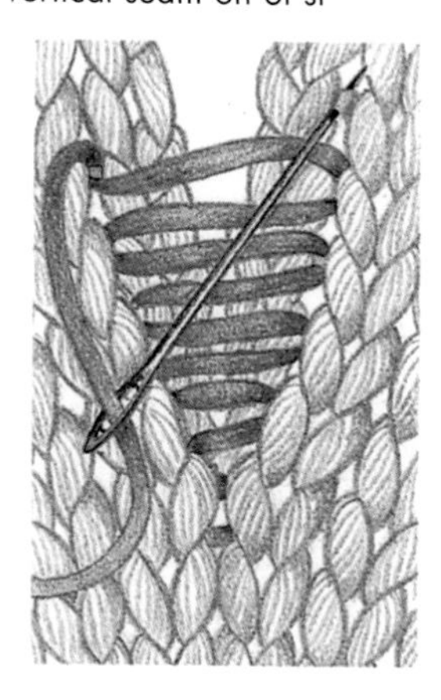

The most common mistake is when you don't go in where you came out. We have a mantra that we recite while sewing to avoid making mistakes: "Go in where you come out and move forward two." Repeating this should help keep you on track. At the end of the row, push the needle through to the wrong side and bury your tail. We like to bury our tails in the seams for additional security.

When working edges that go in different directions, you will be sewing stitches to rows. Watch as you work to be sure that you are working evenly from piece to piece. If necessary, take 2 bars on one side and 1 on the other to evenly assemble the pieces. You are in total control...yeah!

Crocheting Seams

If you don't like sewing and are more comfortable with crochet, you can join the seams in slip stitch. For shoulders, or other horizontal seams, place the pieces together so right sides at facing and bound-off edges are even. Use a crochet hook that's about one or two sizes smaller than your needle size. Insert the hook under both loops on each piece. Remember that a stitch consists of two parts. Place the yarn over the hook and pull a loop through both pieces. Insert the hook under both loops of the next stitch and pull up another loop. Pull the new loop through the original loop so that one loop remains on the hook.

Slip stitch a horizontal seam

Repeat working across the row. Watch as you work to be sure that you are not splitting stitches and not pulling too tightly. At the end of the row, cut yarn leaving a tail, then pull the tail through the stitch on the hook to fasten off. Pull tightly to secure tail. Bury the tail. It's just that easy.

For sides, or other vertical seams, place the pieces together so right sides are facing and side edges are even. Work as for horizontal seams, except you'll be working into rows, instead of stitches.

EDGINGS

Depending on the project, different crochet techniques will be worked on or along the edges to finish them off beautifully. Here are our three favorites.

Single crochet

This stitch adds an additional row to your work and will uncurl the edge. Single crochet is worked from the right to the left across or around the edge.

With the right side facing, insert the crochet hook into the first stitch at the corner or seam. Wrap the yarn over the hook and pull through a loop. Insert hook into next stitch on the row and pull up another loop—two loops are now on the hook.

Step 1 for single crochet—2 loops on hook

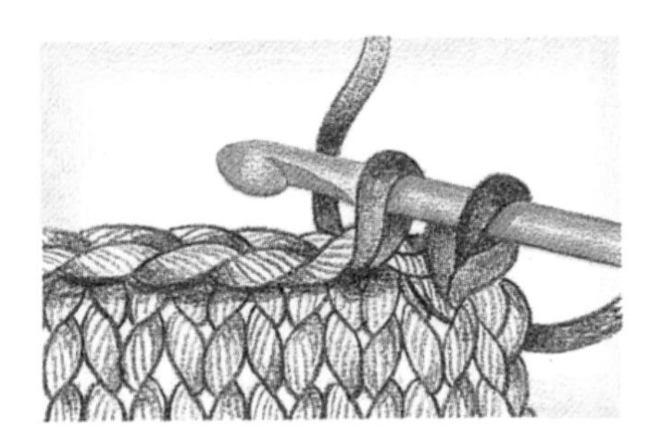

Wrap the yarn over the hook and pull through both loops on the hook—one single crochet stitch is now completed.

Repeat across the row. Because the gauge for single crochet and your knitting gauge will vary, watch carefully as you work. Every few stitches, place your work

Step 2 for single crochet—one sc completed

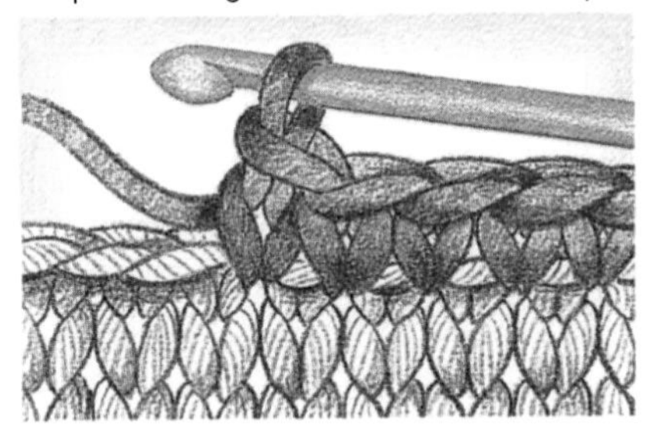

flat and look to see if it is pulling or ruffling. If it is pulling, go up in your crochet hook size and do not pull your stitches too tightly. If it is ruffling, spread out your stitches by skipping a stitch for every three or four stitches that are worked.

Reverse Single Crochet

For some of our designs, we have you work a row of reverse single crochet (also known as crab stitch). There is usually a foundation row of single crochet on which you'll work. Here, you will be working in the opposite direction (from left to right) across the row.

Step 1 for rev single crochet—drawing up a loop

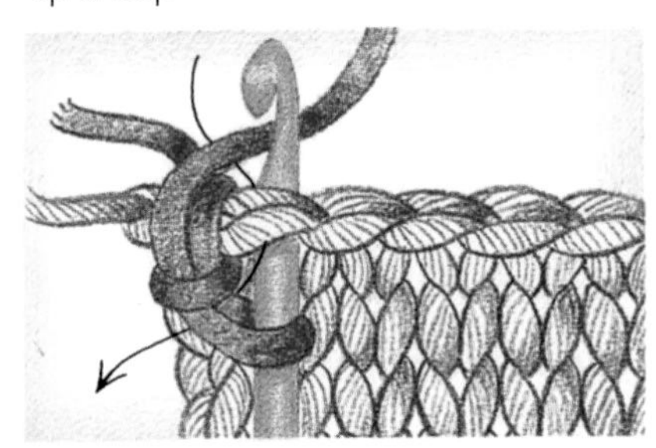

With the right side facing, insert the hook into the stitch all the way at the right. Wrap the yarn over and draw up a loop. You now have 2 loops on the hook. Wrap the yarn over the hook and draw through both loops to finish the stitch.

Repeat across the row. Because you are working in the opposite direction, try to keep your hook parallel with the edge of your knitting. If you find that you are twisting your hand around as you work, the finished stitch will be wrong. This stitch feels awkward at first but gets easier the more you work it.

Step 2 for rev single crochet—drawing through 2 loops on hook

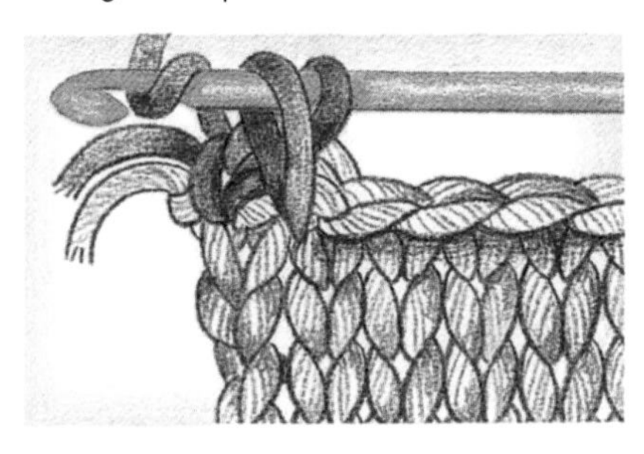

Slip Stitch

We use this technique to flatten out an edge, as well as adding the contrasting color and texture of the Hannah Silk ribbon. While it's done in regular slip stitch, the result is a very pretty chain-stitch accent that looks embroidered. The slip stitch can either be done directly onto the knitted piece, 1 stitch from the edge, or into a base of single crochet stitches. Because it sits on top of the work, it does not add an additional row.

For slip stitch—insert the crochet hook into a stitch, catch the yarn and pull up a loop.

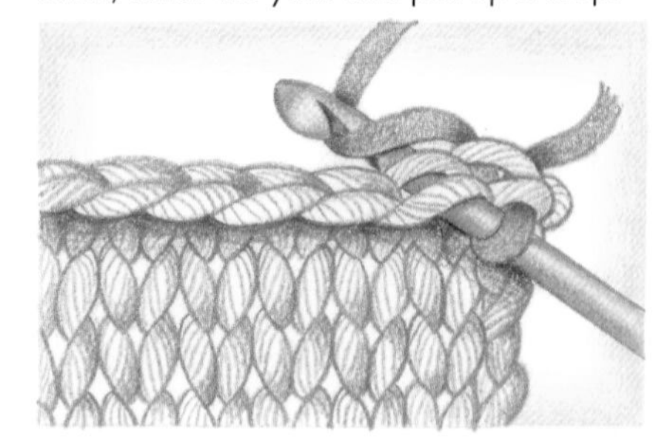

To do, insert the hook under both loops of the corner stitch, then wrap the yarn over the hook.

Pull up a loop, then insert the hook into the next stitch. Wrap the yarn over the hook.

Pull up another stitch, then pull the new stitch through the first stitch in one movement.

Repeat across the row. You must pay careful attention to your tension as this stitch can easily pull too tightly and really gather in the row. If this is an issue, either loosen up your tension or increase your hook one or two sizes.

THE FINAL TOUCH

Once everything is put together, you should give the finished project one final blocking. We have you make seams that are a bit thicker so that the garment will lay firmly on the body. We like it when you wear the garment and not when the garment wears you. For the home décor items, the thicker seams allow for wear and tear.

Turn the entire piece inside out. If you have a body form, put the finished garment on the form. Otherwise, place the piece on a dry, flat surface. Carefully pass light steam over the seams, then give them a little tug to flatten them out and soften them. Make sure that all tails are buried carefully. If the yarn tails are slipping or popping, use a touch of clear nail polish or Fray Check fabric glue to hold them in place.

Jump for joy...you've done it! Your garment is ready to wear or your home décor accessory is ready to display. You should be very proud of yourself. In school we were taught a wonderful phrase: "Simple, clear and logical." We hope that you've enjoyed what you've made and that everything we have shared with you was "Simple, clear and logical."

AFTER CARE

Most knits can be gently hand-washed. If you question how something can be cared for, work with your original knitted swatch. Wash it in the sink and dry it. See how it responds. In some cases, knits can be put in the washing machine. Check your swatch by putting it in a lingerie bag, then washing it through a complete cycle with cold water. It is always best to check your swatch for "wash and wear" issues and not the finished garment.

You should save your yarn labels for future reference along with about a yard/meter of yarn for emergencies. The label usually gives you washing instructions. Because yarn manufacturers cannot go home with you, they will advise you to "Dry Clean." If the label suggests "Dry Clean Only, " please be sure to do that. If the label says "Dry Clean Recommended," then you have options and should work with your swatch to see what you can do. Before taking the plunge, also be sure to have the instructions for the garment and a tape measure to make sure everything measures up to its original size after it is washed.

Hand Washing

When washing by hand, always use a very mild soap that is good for delicates and contains no bleach; never use detergent. The key to successful cleaning is not to destroy or break down the fibers. Hurting the fibers will occur if the water is too warm or the soap is too strong. Put the soap into the water as the sink fills so that the chemicals dissolve evenly. Feel the temperature of the water to make sure it is cool. Turn the garment inside out. Carefully place it at the edge of the sink and allow it to slide down the edge. Never force water through the garment. Move your hand through the water allowing the water to flow through the garment. When ready, move the sweater to one side and allow the water to drain from the sink. Press down gently on the garment to remove excess water. Working in the same manner, but without soap, rinse the garment a few times until the water runs clear and is not soapy.

Carefully support the garment as you remove it from the sink and place it on a dry, flat surface. Open up the garment and spread it out and into shape. At the same time, use a tape measure to form the pieces into their original measurements. Let dry completely.

Machine Washing

If you find that you are able to wash the swatch in the machine, go ahead and do the same for your garment. Always use cool or cold water and be sure that the garment is inside out and in a lingerie bag. Again, watch the soap that you use. It must be mild to avoid shocking the yarn. When the cycle is done, place the bag in a cool dryer and allow the garment to partially dry. Remove the garment and open it up on a dry flat surface. Spread it out and use a tape measure to form the pieces into their original measurements. Let dry completely before wearing. If the knit surface appears a bit matted, run your hands over the fibers allowing them to brush up and become vibrant once again.

ACKNOWLEDGMENTS

We wish to say "Thank You" to many special people who helped make this book possible.

- To Jessie Bear for putting on the finishing touches. We love your blessings.
- To Peggy Yao for taking on the adventure and making it become a reality.
- To Hersick for making peace with some of the pieces.
- To Irene Reiss for believing.
- To Kirstin Muench of Muench Yarns for giving us some of her beautiful yarns. You are the best.
- To Laura Bryant of Prism Arts for adding heavenly hand dyed yarns to our beautiful mix of yarns.....thanks for the friendship.
- To the Hannah Silk Co. for giving all of the luscious dyed silk ribbons that are butterfly tied along the edges of many of our sweaters and accessories.
- To Edna Kohn for knowing that we, Fayla and Barry, needed to be working together.
- To Trisha Malcolm for letting us "pitch" our idea and helping us make it happen.
- To the staff of Sixth&Spring Books for watching over our ideas and helping to see them through.
- To the staff of Trendsetter Yarns for finding the yarns and covering our tracks as we set out to put this book together.
- To the manufacturers of our beautiful yarns...may we continue to create new and exciting yarns and sweaters together...Thanks for your creativity.
- To the retailers who purchase our yarns and patterns...together we make a great team.
- To our sales agents...continue to keep the drive alive.
- Most of all, "love, thanks, gratitude and special hugs" to our families for allowing us to take the time to see this dream come true.

RESOURCES

For a list of shops in your area or for mail order/internet companies that carry the yarns mentioned in this book, write to the following companies or visit their websites.

Fayla Reiss Collection
c/o Trendsetter Yarns
16745 Saticoy St. #101
Van Nuys, Ca. 91406
www.trendsetteryarns.com

Hannah Silk
5155 Myrtle Ave.
Eureka, Ca. 95503

Muench Yarns
1323 Scott St.
Petaluma, Ca. 94954
www.muenchyarns.com

Lane Borgosesia
C/O Trendsetter Yarns
16745 Saticoy St. #101
Van Nuys, Ca. 91406
www.trendsetteryarns.coom

Prism Arts
3140 39th Ave. N
St. Petersburg, Fl. 33714
www.prismyarn.com

Trendsetter Yarns
16745 Saticoy St. #101
Van Nuys, Ca. 91406
www.trendsetteryarns.com

Editorial Director
Trisha Malcolm

Art Director
Chi Ling Moy

Executive Editor
Carla S. Scott

Instructions Editor
Pat Harste

Graphic Designer
Sheena Thomas

Technical Illustrations
Jane Fay

Stylist
Laura Maffeo

Book Division Manager
Erica Smith

Production Manager
David Joinnides

Photography
Jack Deutsch Studios

President, Sixth&Spring Books
Art Joinnides